Theatre Semiotics

Advances in Semiotics

THOMAS A. SEBEOK, GENERAL EDITOR

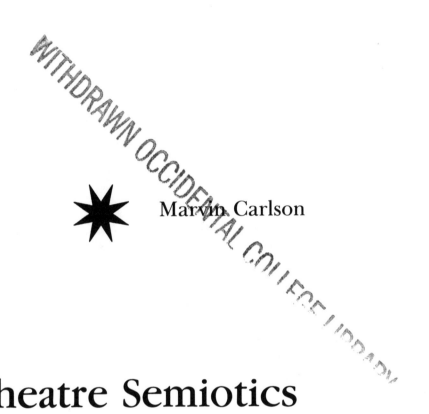

Marvin Carlson

Theatre Semiotics

Signs of Life

Indiana University Press / Bloomington and Indianapolis

Manufactured in the United States of America

Library of Congress Cataloging-in-Publication Data

Theatre Semiotics: Signs of Life   /
  Marvin Carlson.
     p. cm.
   Includes index.
   ISBN 0–253–31315–5
   1. Theater—Semiotics.   I. Carlson, Marvin A.
PN2041.S45S54   1990
792' .0141—dc19   89–45193
                                                       CIP

1 2 3 4 5 93 92 91 90 89

*To Bert States, in appreciation of the
nourishing crops he has gathered in
some of these same fields*

The richest collection of semical facts seems indeed to be that produced by the performance of an opera. The artists communicate with the audience in a variety of ways: through words, music, mime, dance, the costumes of the actors; through the music of the orchestra, the setting and the lighting onstage and in the auditorium; through the architecture of the theatre. The audience communicates with the artists through its various reactions. Members of the audience communicate with each other through words and the various actions of everyday life. Then one must not forget the theatre personnel such as the firemen and police. In short, a whole world here gathers and communicates for the length of several hours.

Eric Buyssens
Les langages et le discours

CONTENTS

INTRODUCTION   xi

PART ONE *The Rules of the Game*   1

   Semiotics and Nonsemiotics in Performance   3
   Theatre Audiences and the Reading of Performance   10
   The Semiotics of Character Names in the Drama   26

PART TWO *The Playing Field*   39

   The Semiotics of Theatre Structures   41
   The Old Vic: A Semiotic Analysis   56
   The Iconic Stage   75

PART THREE **Audience Improvisation**   93

   Psychic Polyphony   95
   Local Semiosis and Theatrical Interpretation   110

INDEX   123

Introduction

The essays gathered in this collection have appeared in a variety of places and from a variety of inspirations. Some were stimulated by the reflections of other writers on the theatre, some grew from striking experiences in the theatre itself that seemed to call for explanation or exploration, and some arose from tantalizing loose ends left in previous essays. As they have been written, over a period now of almost a decade, both my own interests in the possible application of semiotic methods to theatre analysis and that field itself have undergone constant change, largely in the direction of ever-greater richness and complexity. Nevertheless, sufficient common concerns inform these essays, I believe, to make the gathering of them in a single place for mutual enhancement justifiable.

The reader with some acquaintance with semiotically oriented theatre research, especially in America, will find these essays have a rather different orientation from much such work, but one that I hope will be seen as both illuminating and stimulating. In the late 1970s, when a number of studies in theatre semiotics became available in English, the field, which had been rapidly developing in Europe during the previous decade, had recently undergone an important change in emphasis, one that brought it more closely into line with the long-neglected writings of the pioneers of theatre semiotics early in the century who were members of the Prague Linguistic Circle.

Between the mid-1960s and the mid-1970s in Europe, the dominant tools of analysis utilized by those investigating the semiotics of the theatre were derived from the methods of structural linguistics and communication theory, supplemented by such closely related literary strategies as narratology. Such analysis spoke often of theatrical signs, signifying units, and codes, but the major source of information about these constructs tended to be sought in literary texts. In this these semiotic theorists followed the traditional emphasis of Western theatrical theory, considering performance as distinctly ancillary to the written script. Traditional logocentrism and the assumption that the authorial vision was transparent in the written text was part of the motive for this. (Charles Lamb, Goethe, and Pirandello are among the many who have regarded theatrical performance as a derived and necessarily inferior version of the written text.) Surely equally important, however, were the more practical concerns that the written text was a more permanent and accessible object of study, and, as a verbal structure, was more immediately open to the tools already developed for the analysis of narrative and of discourse.

In the late 1970s, however, Marco de Marinis in Italy and others urged with ever-growing success that theatre semiotics must give more attention to performance as an important "text" in its own right.[1] Thus the first important studies on the subject in English, such as Kier Elam's, appearing soon after, placed much emphasis upon approaches such as kinesics, proxemics, and paralinguistics, in hopes that these might provide the tools for analyzing the "spectacle text."[2] In fact only a small amount of such work has been done, either on performance tradition in general or on specific productions, and that has been done primarily by European scholars such as Erika Fischer-Lichte, Tadeusz Kowzan, and Patrice Pavis. The actual literary text/spectacle text relationship has inspired a fairly substantial body of writing in English, and a number of more abstract speculations on the semiotics of theatre in general, but the majority of writing on this subject continues to focus primarily on the written text, with occasional reflection upon its scenic realization.

Whether such writing looks to the page, the stage, or the relationship between the two, there is a common preoccupation with the production of signs and, moreover, with the production of a certain group of signs: those found in the written text and those found in the realization of that text in a particular performance. The concept of theatre underlying such approaches might be summarized by Roland Barthes' well-known and succinct semiotic definition of theatre. In response to a question from the journal *Tel Quel,* Barthes characterized the theatre as "a kind of cybernetic machine" which, as soon as the curtain rises, sends out a variety of simultaneous messages (from setting, costume, and lighting, as well as from the positions, words, and gestures of the actors), some of which remain constant for extended periods (such as the setting), while others continuously change (such as words and gestures).[3]

In my own consideration of theatre from a semiotic perspective, I found this sort of model very helpful at first, and still find it helpful to a degree, but I gradually became more and more troubled by important aspects of the theatre experience that it largely neglected. Although I found concepts and strategies in semiotic writings that suggested fresh and, in my opinion, more holistic ways of looking at the theatre experience, the great majority of semiotic writing on this subject continued to explore useful but well-worn paths. Increasingly I came to feel that three broad areas of investigation deserved particular attention. Each seemed to me to have great importance in the functioning of theatre as an art form and as a human activity; each had inspired some, but comparatively little, consideration in theatre semiotics to date; and yet each appeared highly accessible to analysis from a semiotic point of view.

The first of these was the contribution of the audience. One might reasonably assume that semiotics, with its historically close connections to discourse and communication, would naturally be as concerned with the reception as with the production of signs; but, at least insofar as the theatre is concerned, this has obviously not been the case. The vast majority of the writings on this subject in fact concern themselves almost

exclusively with the process of sign production by playwright or by production (as we see, for example, in Barthes' definition), and the public,
often not even mentioned, is clearly considered an essentially passive
receiver of this activity.

Interest in this rather neglected area seems to be growing. During the
1980s a number of theorists—some by extending traditional lines of
investigation in semiotics; some by combining semiotic concerns with
insights gained from post-structuralist or reader-response analysis—
have paid much closer attention to the active contribution of the audience. The final chapters of Anne Ubersfeld's *L'école du spectateur* (1982)
provided important impetus for such concerns, developed further in a
special issue of *VS* in 1985 on "Semiotica della ricezione teatrale," and
in a number of illuminating articles by Marco de Marinis, Patrice Pavis,
and others.[4] Not all of this work has been positive. The growing interest
in the process of reception has encouraged a number of "empirical"
audience analyses seriously flawed by methodolical naiveté,[5] but on the
whole this interest has been for me both appropriate and stimulating.

Although the semiotics of audience reception seems to be gaining in
research interest, another related area of potential investigation remains
almost totally unexplored. This is the semiotics of the entire theatre
experience (as opposed to what happens on the stage or between the
on-stage creation and the spectator). We have all too often taken literally
Barthes' comment that the "cybernetic machine" of theatre begins its
operation "as soon as the curtain rises," ceasing, of course, when the
curtain descends. So long as we think of the theatre performance primarily as a discrete artifact for analysis, the problems with this approach
may not be readily apparent, but when we begin to consider the audience
experience of the theatrical event, we should soon come to realize that
the actual performance of the play is only a part (and historically not
always the most important part) of an entire social and cultural experience, and that the "cybernetic machine" by no means begins operating
when the curtain rises, assuming there even is a curtain.

The physical appearance of the auditorium, the displays in the lobby,
the information in the program, and countless other parts of the event
as a whole are also part of its semiotic, and it is a rare production indeed
that does not build at least some of these into the overall impression it
seeks to make upon its audience. No more stimulating expression of the
challenge and potential of a semiotics of the theatre has ever come to
my attention than that of Eric Buyssens in 1943, when such study had
scarcely even begun. Buyssens suggested that operatic performance offered the richest object for semiotic analysis within the entire culture,
since it involved not only the communication of words, music, gesture,
and the visual arts, but social relationships and even the personnel of
the theatre, such as ushers and police, in what Buyssens called "an entire
world."[6] In *Contemporary Aesthetics* Matthew Lippman, though speaking

of the experience of art in general, makes an observation that seems to me particularly relevant to theatre. It should not be assumed, Lippman warns, that the primary subject matter of aesthetics is the so-called art object or the perceiving subject, even though these topics can be legitimately discussed. The focus of concern, Lippman suggests, might more properly be on the aesthetic event as a whole.[7]

Both Buyssens' conception of the theatrical world and Lippman's idea of art as event encourage us to look beyond the essential but limited concerns of the dramatic script and its scenic realization to many neglected elements of the theatre experience—the physical surroundings of the spectators, the structuring of intermissions, the function of programs, and such transitional phenomena as overtures and curtain calls—in short, on every element of the event as a whole that is utilized in the way the spectator experiences and makes sense of this event. Among these many elements, I have been particularly interested in exploring some of the implications of the spectator's physical surroundings, drawing where possible on the work of architectural and urban semiotics, looking not only at the auditorium itself, but also at the entire theatre organization of space and, indeed, at how the placement of the theatre within a city conditions the experience undergone there.

A third area in fact looks to one of the most ancient concerns of theatrical theory, but one which has not so far inspired extended speculation among theatre semioticians, and that is the relation of theatre to the life of which it is an imitation. Much has been written of theatrical codes and signs, and much of the relationship between the codes and signs of the written text and of the performance text, but much less of the relationship that is more central to theatre than to any other art: the relationship between the signs and codes of theatre and those of everyday life. Elam and others have rightly called attention to the major importance of iconicity in the theatre, of signs that in the definition of Peirce are "like" those things they represent.[8]

Elam usefully notes that in the theatre iconicity regularly appears in its most extreme form, when an element in the production is not merely "like" the thing it represents, but is in fact the same thing or at least the same *kind* of thing. Thus a chair represents a chair and a glove, a glove, but also gestures, movements, words—the whole communicative machinery of our cultural life—appear on stage in a form frequently indistinguishable from how they appear in daily life, a phenomenon Elam calls "iconic identity."[9] The centrality of this phenomenon naturally encourages audiences to utilize extratheatrical codes to understand and interpret what they experience in the theatre, to a greater degree than in any other art form. This is surely one of the great sources of the power of the theatre, but it also makes the theatre peculiarly susceptible to audience responses based on assumptions developed outside the art. Rather than attempt to limit this indeterminacy by emphasizing its own internal codes and systems of meaning, the theatre, especially in the West, has historically sought new power and stimulus by continually absorbing the raw material of everyday life.

This process and its theoretical implications have attracted more attention among phenomenologists than semioticians, and Bert States has provided the best discussion of it I have so far encountered,[10] but much more seems to me to need exploration along these lines, both phenomenologically and semiotically. What is the relationship between our interpretation of stage objects, gestures, and actions, and seemingly almost identical objects, gestures, and actions outside the theatre? How is the theatre affected by its relatively high reliance upon externally generated codes, whose operation and interpretation usually lie totally beyond the art form that utilizes them? How is the interpretive situation itself established and/or controlled? André Antoine, the pioneer of realism, placed chairs from his mother's living room on stage. The Antoines of today may invite audiences into the living room itself, placing both audiences and chairs in a considerably more ambiguous and intriguing interpretive situation. Most of these concerns, it will be noted, return in one way or another to the experience of the audience—what it brings to the theatre, and how it organizes and understands what it finds there. In semiotic terms, what I have been pursuing seems to me best described in Peirce's discussion of the interpretant.

Peirce is careful to distinguish, as many semiotic theorists are not, between the sign itself and what the sign stimulates in the mind of the interpreter. This result of the sign Peirce calls the interpretant, and as usual he considers it in three aspects: the immediate, the dynamic, and the final. In brief, the immediate is the innate interpretability of the sign before it reaches the interpreter, a potential meaning; and the final is the ultimate interpretation, a kind of Aristotelian complete form reached when all possible considerations have been assimilated. One of these two abstract aspects has usually been taken for granted as the "meaning" of the sign, especially in semiotic studies of theatre and drama, reinforced, if necessary, by the assumption that *this* meaning is what the author (or artist) "intended." But Peirce's second aspect, the dynamic, brings us much closer to the actual experience of theatre. In a letter to Lady Welby, Peirce defines this as "that which is experienced in each act of Interpretation and is different in each from that of any other." Later he calls the dynamical interpretant "a single actual event."[11] The analysis of this experience, this event, inasmuch as can be discovered of its totality, seems to me the most challenging and the most worthwhile task now facing theatre semiotics, and it is my hope that each of the following essays, in one way or another, may contribute to that task.

Although all of these essays involve to some extent these interlocking concerns of the dynamics of the total theatre event, the contribution of the audience to the semiotic process, and the peculiar quality of reality in the theatre, I have attempted to arrange them to emphasize certain closely related concerns and perspectives. The first group, "The Rules of the Game," is the most traditional in approach, since its emphasis is on the created theatrical object offered to an audience and some of the ways in which that object (and its surroundings) both provide material for an audience to interpret and suggest rules for its interpretation.

The first essay, "Semiotics and NonSemiotics in Theatre," seeks to demonstrate on the most basic level how this process continues to work in the theatre, even in situations designed to prevent it from working. This essay originally appeared in *Modern Drama* and was stimulated by an early essay in that journal by Michael Kirby, outlining his theory and practice in creating what he considered to be a nonsemiotic theatre. I have always found Kirby provocative and stimulating, both as a theatre practitioner and as a theorist, even when, as in this case, I have not agreed with him. The question of whether, or under what circumstances, the theatre might free itself from the semiotic process involved a number of basic considerations that I think may serve as a useful preparation for the subsequent essays.

"Theatre Audiences and the Reading of Performance" is one of a series of essays by contemporary theatre scholars gathered by Thomas Postlewait and Bruce McConachie under the title *Interpreting the Theatrical Past* (Iowa City, 1989). The goal of this collection is to provide suggestions about how various recent critical and theoretical methodologies might be utilized to offer fresh insights and fresh strategies in the study of theatre history. As will have been clear from what I have already said, my particular concerns in theatre semiotics have necessarily overlapped the closely related critical fields of reader-response and reception theory. This essay maps out some of that common terrain insofar as it might encourage some new directions in theatre historiography.

The third essay, "The Semiotics of Character Names in the Drama," appeared in *Semiotica* 44 (1983). It is the most specific in this section, tracing the workings of a specific type of narrative coding through the range of Western drama and as adjusted for changing interpretive communities. In this respect it may be considered an elaboration on one aspect of the previous essay.

The second group of essays, "The Playing Field," pursues a concern I have found particularly interesting, which grew directly out of Buyssens' proposal for a total semiotic study of the performance situation. These essays consider a major part of that situation: the space in which the performance occurs. The opening essay in this section, "The Semiotics of Theatre Structures," seeks to provide an introduction to this subject, outlining a range of possible analytic strategies. It has never appeared in this form, though it combines material from two papers, one presented at the ATA convention in San Francisco in 1984 and the other at the Conference on the Semiotics of Opera held at Royaumont,

France, that same fall. The Royaumont paper was published as "The Semiotics of Opera Structures" in the conference proceedings, *Approches de l'opéra* (Paris, 1986). The book *Places of Performance* (Cornell, 1989) developed from the concerns in these papers.

"The Old Vic: A Semiotic Analysis" (*Semotica*, 1988) demonstrates the application of this sort of analysis to a single theatre, one with a particularly rich and varied social and cultural history, and one, therefore, that has been involved diachronically with an intriguing variety of interpretive communities. "The Iconic Stage," from *The Journal of Dramatic Theory and Criticism* (forthcoming), provides a very different perspective, considering the semiotics not of a traditional performance location, such as the Old Vic, but of nontheatrical spaces appropriated for performance because of other extratheatrical meanings associated with them.

The final section, "Audience Improvisation," looks directly at the semiotics of theatre reception and at some of the particular ways in which theatre audiences contribute to the creation of the "meaning" of the theatre event. These deal most directly with Peirce's dynamic interpretant as it operates in the theatre. The first essay in this section, "Psychic Polyphony," is in large part the same article that appeared under that title in *The Journal of Dramatic Theory and Criticism* in the fall of 1986, but I have added to it some very closely related material from another article, "The Theatre Event and Film Documentation" (*Dégres* 48, Winter 1986). The multiplicity and simultaneity of theatrical stimuli have been noted by many theatre semioticians, but this is, I believe, the first attempt to consider in some detail the implications of this for the way a theatre audience makes sense of what is happening on stage.

Finally, "Local Semiosis and Theatrical Interpretation," first presented at a conference on local semiosis at the University of Rochester in April of 1987, turns from audience interpretation of specific works to some more general implications of interpretation in the theatre, particularly as the theatrical work is experienced by different interpretive communities. Any work of art, as it reaches different audiences, will inevitably be perceived in somewhat different ways. But the theatrical performance participates in this process in a particularly active way, since it reaches its audience only through an intervening interpretation (of the written text), one that because of the complexity of the medium is far more open than, for example, the interpretation of a musical score. Buyssens advanced operatic performance as the culture's most challenging object for semiotic analysis on the grounds that it offered "the richest combination of semical facts." Certainly one should add to this the related point that this rich combination is in constant flux, since theatre lives only in the ephemeral performance and each new performance necessarily creates a whole new constellation of elements.

If the dazzling complexity of the messages generated by the theatre event provides semioticians with one of their greatest analytic challenges, even more challenging is the richness of interpretative possibilities opened by the constant and inevitable mutability of signs in performance. No other art seeks to absorb and convert into interpretive structures so much of the total human experience as the theatre does, its potential resources and meanings bounded only by the resources and meanings of humanity itself. Such are the richness and the challenge of the theatre's signs of life.

NOTES

1. Marco de Marinis, "Lo spettacolo come testo 1, 2," *VS* 21, 22 (September–December 1978 and January–April 1979).

2. Kier Elam, *The Semiotics of Theatre and Drama* (London, 1980).

3. Roland Barthes, *Critical Essays*, trans. Richard Howard (Evanston, 1972), 261–62.

4. See the citations to my essay "Theatre Audiences and the Reading of Performance."

5. I have discussed this problem, with specific examples, in two review articles in *Semiotica*: "Contemporary Concerns in the Semiotics of Theatre," 48-3/4 (1984), 281–91, and "Analytical Theatre Theory: Reality and Illusion," 62-3/4 (1968), 365–71.

6. Eric Buyssens, *Les languages et le discours* (Brussels, 1943), 56.

7. Matthew Lippman, *Contemporary Aesthetics* (Boston, 1973), 3.

8. C. S. Peirce, *Collected Papers* (Cambridge, 1931–58), v. 2, par. 247.

9. Elam, *Semiotics*, 22–23.

10. Bert O. States, *Great Reckonings in Little Rooms: On the Phenomenology of Theatre*, especially the chapter "The World on Stage" (Berkeley, 1985), 19–47.

11. Peirce, *Semiotics and Significs*, ed. C. S. Hardwick (Bloomington, 1977), 111.

PART ONE

The Rules of the Game

✳ ✳ ✳ ✳ ✳   Semiotics and
Nonsemiotics in
Performance

THE INCREASING IMPORTANCE of theoretical considerations in contemporary American drama and theatre was reflected by a special issue of *Modern Drama* in 1982 devoted to theory and performance. In that issue experimental director and theorist Michael Kirby described in some detail a type of performance in which he had recently been engaged. This approach Kirby characterized by the name "structuralist," and it was presented by him as an attempt at a "nonsemiotic" performance experience. This attempt to drive a wedge between structuralism and semiotics doubtless came as something of a surprise to many readers who were aware of the close relationship historically between these terms, so close indeed that Jonathan Culler, in one of the central modern works on structuralism in literature, could observe, "It would not be wrong to suggest that structuralism and semiology are identical."[1] Perhaps equally surprising, at a time when semiotics seemed to be developing as the most promising new theoretical approach to the full range of text and performance analysis, Kirby's argument sought to locate an important type of experimental performance entirely outside the range of such analysis.

This challenge to the general applicability of semiotic analysis, an applicability normally taken for granted by semioticians, offers a useful starting point for the consideration of the procedures and the claims of such analysis. The determination of whether a nonsemiotic theatre is possible and what its characteristics might be should prove of considerable help in understanding, by contrast, just what semiotic analysis of performance involves, what sort of assumptions support it, what it may be expected to accomplish, and what sort of phenomena do in fact lie outside its domain.

The major part of Kirby's article on nonsemiotic performance deals with the creation and presentation of his "structuralist" or "nonsemiotic" work, entitled *Double Gothic*. Were one simply to read the description of this performance without its author's accompanying explanation, the use of the term "nonsemiotic" would surely seem puzzling and problematic, since the performance seems to be composed almost entirely of elements that would normally be considered semiotic. In one scene where "The Heroine meets the Helper of the Antagonist," the scene is thus described: "Apparently she has gotten off a train expecting someone to meet her, but nobody is there. Rain threatens; a dog howls. Then a blind woman appears, apparently sent by 'the doctor.'" A parallel scene ends with "thunder and lightning." Surely signification is constantly involved here, even if these scenes are composed of nothing more than fleeting images. The "doctor" mentioned in this passage subsequently appears, an actress dressed in "a white lab coat and rubber gloves"—clearly signs of that profession. The character relationships, derived from the actantial models of Propp, seem hardly likely to help free the play from semiotics, as Kirby hopes, but rather develop another semiotic element—that of the culturally supported morphology of character relationships from which the "Heroine," "Helper," and "Antagonist" are derived. The "Gothic" elements found everywhere in the play (and it its title) provide further semiotic material, derived from generic expectations, even when the performance plays consciously against those expectations.

Upon what grounds, then, can *Double Gothic* be proposed as an example of "nonsemiotic" performance? To respond to this, one must begin with the working definition of semiotics provided by Kirby near the beginning of his discussion of this experimental work: "I take semiotic analysis to be based upon a model of art-as-communication. In this model, there is a sender, a message (encoded by the sender), and a receiver (who decodes—at least to some degree—the message). Semiotics can be seen to deal primarily with this process of decoding the encoded message."[2] Of course, the first thing that will strike anyone who has read much of the work in modern semiotic theory is that this definition is an extremely narrow one. It is essentially a strict application of a highly simplified linguistic communication model, quite unacceptable to semiotic theorists who approach the subject (as most Americans do) from a more general perspective such as that of Peirce, regarding the communication model as only one out of many semiotic possibilities.

I shall return presently to the question of whether nonsemiotic performance can be conceived in the light of these broader theoretic perspectives, but for the moment let us remain with the communication model Kirby proposes, considering the implications of a nonsemiotic performance within the terms of this definition. The basic strategy of *Double Gothic* is fairly straightforward. If semiotics can be defined as the sending of a message by means of an intermediate code system understood by sender and receiver, one need only refuse to send a message, leaving the code (here, the performance) without a content. This strategy, apparently simple, nevertheless presents a number of possible difficulties, some involving the sender, some the medium, and some the receiver. Kirby is well aware of these and explains a number of steps taken to overcome them. The sender may in the manipulation of the medium send a message unconsciously, but Kirby argues that this difficulty can be prevented by a continuing commitment to avoid sending any such message during the careful screening that goes on during the rehearsal process. The medium itself may contain communicative elements (such as the codified elements already noted, the "doctor's" coat for example), but these do not in Kirby's analysis make the performance "semiotic" because they do not add up to a coherent "message." Finally the receiver, the audience, may think it perceives a message even when none was intended. Kirby recognizes that this possibility is always present but argues that what is involved here is not semiotic, since we are dealing not with communication but with interpretation. He recalls Eco's observation that acts of "inference" should not be considered semiotic acts unless they are "culturally recognized and systematically coded."[3]

Theatre semioticians may recognize echoes here of the most famous argument for a nonsemiotic view of theatre, that of Georges Mounin in his *Introduction à la sémiologie,* though Mounin took a much more extreme view than Kirby's, rejecting the communication model for *all* theatre. The transmitting of a message, even when this occurred, was of far less importance to him than the function of the theatre as a stimulus seeking to arouse the very complicated response in the spectators known as the aesthetic experience.[4] Kirby seeks a similar complex response rather than communication, the creation of "new emotions" through exposure to the way the mind works to make connections.

Mounin's approach, however, has been consistently rejected by subsequent semiotic theorists, who have argued that no spectator can respond emotionally or aesthetically to a theatre performance without some understanding of what is happening, and that this understanding can occur only by a semiotic process involving the utilization of cultural codes.[5] A similar response could be made, it seems, to the designation of *Double Gothic* as nonsemiotic. Though we are in theory involved here with a process rather than a message, that process, like Mounin's aesthetic experience, is developed from elements participating in semiosis. The lab coat, the howling dog, the threatening rain, and so on are not separated from the "culturally recognized" codes Eco associates with the semiotic process. They bear messages, even if these do not add up to any specific overarching message.

Nor is this the only semiotic dimension of the elements in *Double Gothic*. Quite aside from this sort of general culturally encoded message, the elements are offered in a mimetic context not apparently different, in this respect, from traditional theatre. The actress who plays the blind woman is not, it seems, truly blind; the thunder is not real, but produced during the performance in some mechanical manner; and so on. The audience, in turn, is quite aware of these conventions, long accepted as the basis of theatrical illusion. But here again we are in the realm of the semiotic. If the thunder is not real thunder, and if the blind woman is not a real blind woman, then they appear as iconic representatives of those realities, in short as signs.

An awareness of this all-pervasive iconicity of theatre may be found from the very beginnings of dramatic theory, in the Greek concept of mimesis. Although Plato and Aristotle drew very different conclusions, they agreed that theatre was based upon imitation, that its elements stood for an absent reality. Bogatyrev and others in the Prague Circle stressed that this imitation, or signification, operated not only with the action, as Aristotle noted, but with every element of performance. A stove in a production of *Hedda Gabler* may be a real stove, as the actress playing Hedda is a real human being, but these also, by the conventions of mimesis, serve as signs for the "absent, real" Hedda and her "absent, real" furniture, even before the more complex connotative significations begin.

There seems only one possible way to remove this semiotic dimension of the performance medium, and that would be to remove the entire element of mimesis. So radical an operation would take us outside the realm of theatre as it has traditionally been conceived, but not outside that of recent performance experimentation. Let us, for example, suppose that instead of an actress playing Hedda Gabler, burning Lövborg's manuscript, we offer the audience a woman, not in character, simply performing the action of burning papers in a stove. What we are then offering is something akin to a happening, one of the central features of which is precisely the absence of mimesis. Kirby's continuing interest in a performance freed from a communication model clearly owes something to his interest in the mid-1960s in happenings and related experimentation. Indeed, his distinction in 1965 between happenings and traditional theatre bears a close resemblance to his more recent distinction between structuralist, or nonsemiotic, and traditional theatre. The happening he called a group of elements arranged according to a "private scheme" of the artist, while traditional theatre offered an "information structure" accessible to the spectator.[6]

In the calculated rejection of mimetic elements in its medium, the happening may seem closer to a truly nonsemiotic performance than an event like *Double Gothic,* but even if this rejection resulted in a nonsemiotic medium, there would remain semiotic implications still to be dealt with in the sender and receiver. Both were touched upon in an interveiw with John Cage in a special issue of *The Drama Review* devoted to the happening in 1965. In respect to the sender, Cage took issue with Kirby's distinction between an artist's private scheme and an accessible information structure, warning that any sort of intentionality on the part of the artist tended to lead back eventually to the traditional transmission of a message to the public.[7] The only certain way to avoid this, Cage insisted, was by replacing any intentionality, even private, with improvisation and chance.

The participation of the receiver in semiosis was touched upon several times in this interview, most directly in Richard Schechner's question to Cage: "How do you take into account the fact that people, as soon as they become an audience, demand structure and impose it even if it's not there?"[8] Happening theory provided no clear response to this question, and this lack of response is hardly surprising, since we are concerned here with semiosis on the most basic phenomenological level. The very fact that a happening, or any performance, is offered to an audience as an event set off in some way from the naturally occurring events of real life ensures that if the audiences recognize this process at all, they will view the performance as a construct, and thus attempt at once to apply tentative "readings" to it, just as they do universally with culturally generated objects. Although the creator of a happening places within the performance space people, objects, and actions devoid of traditional dramatic matrices, the ostending, or presenting of them in a "showing" situation, guarantees this result. Even if the artist resigned to chance the objects or actions being ostended, the audiences' response would be the same, since they are responding not to the elements being presented, but to the presentation of them within the frame of performance expectations. Such a frame, observes Eco in his essay "Semiotics of Theatrical Performance," imposes semiotic pertinence on both objects and actions, "even though they are not intentional behavior nor non-artificial items."[9] Bruce Wilshire reports precisely such an effect in Robert Whitman's *Light Touch.* The audience is seated inside a warehouse, and a loading door, framed by curtains, is opened onto the street. The creation of this "frame" endows the chance events and objects outside with new significance. The interpretation of signs is of course culturally generated, but so is the recognition of signs *as* signs, and this semiotic dimension seems impossible to avoid in any performance in our culture recognized as a performance by an audience.

This observation suggests, however, another possible strategy for a nonsemiotic performance, which would be the creation of a performance not recognized as such by its audience, and thus not open to the usual interpretive process of the performance situation. An example of performance of this type may be found in the "invisible theatre" of the Latin American theorist and director Augusto Boal. "Invisible theatre" is presented in nontheatrical spaces for a public unaware of it as theatre. In one such performance, an actress in a market pretends to be illiterate and expresses fear that a merchant is cheating her. A second actress checks the figures, finds them correct, and informs the first of the advantages and procedures of enrolling in a local literacy course, all this for the benefit of the bystanders. In another scenario, actors in a restaurant pretending to be regular patrons expose to other diners the inequities between the wages paid to workers and the prices charged for special dinners.[10]

Clearly, however, we cannot characterize the "invisible theatre" as nonsemiotic, even though it has abolished the performance frame and the audience apprehension of ostentation (the scenes are ostended, but are not supposed to be recognized as such). We have, as the basis of this theatre, not only a very specific concern with message communication, but also an elaborate semiotic process for the bearing of that message. Eco has suggested that the stage actor is constantly involved with two levels of speech acts, the first a performative statement ("I am acting") and the second the pseudostatements of the character portrayed.[11] In the "invisible theatre," the actors also make a performative statement, but here a false one ("I am not performing"). In both cases, this statement is supported by an appropriate frame, but the actors of the "invisible theatre" cannot rely entirely upon the frame of marketplace or restaurant to support their action. They must also follow the cultural codes of appropriate behavior in these locales, at least to the extent that they will be interpreted by their spectators as village women or diners rather than as actors. Only if this process is established can the step actually desired by director and actors be taken, when the spectator, though unaware of the actors as actors, comes to recognize that their interaction may be seen as the sign of a social problem or social reality. The specific removal of a performance semiotic has by no means removed these events from the semiotic process.

Kirby's simplified communication model of semiosis, based upon early linguistic theory, with a clearly defined sender, message, and receiver, is obviously inadequate to deal with the range of theatre and performance possibilities; but when we consider semiosis in more general terms, with this model as only one specialized case, we soon come to realize that performance, since it is realized within a culture, can hardly escape it. Barthes pointed out in *Elements of Semiology* the virtual impossibility of creating a nonsignifying object in any society, since there is no reality except what is intelligible, and as social beings we structure our intelligible universe according to the semiotic systems of our culture.[12] We have seen that experiments removing intentionality from the sender, meanings from the message, or a performance frame from the audience have in no case thereby produced a truly nonsemiotic performance. Indeed, it is difficult to imagine and perhaps impossible to describe just what such a performance would be like, since we could talk or think about it only with the tools provided by our culture. One would have to imagine an experience created entirely by chance, involving elements bearing no meaning, and perceived by audiences whose culture provided them with no way of making sense of this experience. The result might be something like the "one great blooming, buzzing confusion" that William James postulates as the experience of the newborn baby before any differentiation of experiential phenomena has begun.[13] But whatever this experience would be like if it could be created, we would probably call it that—an "experience," or perhaps an "event"—but I think it most unlikely that we would consider "performance" an adequate term.

NOTES

1. Jonathan Culler, (Ithaca, 1975), 6.
2. Michael Kirby, "Nonsemiotic Performance," *Modern Drama* 25 (March 1982), 105.
3. Umberto Eco, *A Theory of Semiotics* (Bloomington, 1976), 17.
4. Georges Mounin, *Introduction à la sémiologie* (Paris, 1970), 92–93.
5. See, for example, Anne Ubersfeld, *Lire le théâtre* (Paris, 1978), 40–42, and André Helbo, "Le théâtre: une communication en déni?", *Études littéraires*, 13 (December 1980), 461–70.
6. Kirby, *Happenings[:] An Illustrated Anthology* (New York, 1965), 21.
7. Kirby and Richard Schechner, "An Interview with John Cage," *The Drama Review*, 10 (Winter 1965), 69.
8. Ibid., 57–58.
9. Umberto Eco, "Semiotics of Theatrical Performance," *TDR*, 21 (March 1977), 113.
10. Augusto Boal, *Theatre of the Oppressed*, trans. C.A. and M.O.L. McBride (New York, 1979), 144–47.
11. Eco, "Semiotics," 115.
12. Roland Barthes, *Elements of Semiology*, trans. A. Lavers and C. Smith (London, 1967), 41–42.
13. William James, *The Principles of Psychology*, 2 vols. (New York, 1890), I, 488.

✳ ✳ ✳ ✳ ✳   Theatre Audiences
and the Reading
of Performance

READER-RESPONSE AND RECEPTION theory have now become a thriving new area in the crowded field of contemporary literary speculation, but so far the strategies and concerns of such theory have stimulated comparatively little work in theatre study in general and in historical theatre study in particular.[1] This somewhat surprising situation is unfortunate for both theatre study and reception theory, since theatrical performance, as a uniquely structured event for a circumscribed and often clearly identifiable body of receivers, presents a kind of controlled field of study quite different from the usual literary concerns of reception theory, since this theory may offer to theatre research a different way of considering traditional material, leading to new insights into that material.

Despite the much more obvious participation and contribution of the "reader" to the theatrical event than to the novel or poem, much theatre theory still regards the theatre performance as something created and set before an essentially passive audience. Our histories speak of plays or parts of plays directed toward certain audiences or parts of audiences (Shakespeare's jokes to amuse the groundlings, or Lillo's morality lesson for London apprentices), or of conventions that historical audiences somehow learned to accept (masks in the Greek theatre, the invisible Japanese prop man, the Elizabethan boy actresses), but these are almost invariably presented as features of the performance or play to which an audience passively responds. Little is said about how that audience learns to respond to such matters or what demands and contributions of its own it brings to the event.

The rather extensive reader-response and reception bibliography of the past decade or so suggests a number of potentially useful strategies for analyzing contemporary and historical theatre experience. We might consider, for example, the process of concretization as discussed by Wolfgang Iser—the process by which, according to Iser, a reader serves as co-producer of the meaning of a text by creatively filling gaps (*Leerstellen*) left in that text by the author.[2] Those familiar with recent semiotic theatre theory may recall that Anne Ubersfeld has described the dramatic text in a similar way, as *troué*—that is, containing gaps, in this case to be filled by performance.[3]

An interesting parallel is suggested by this convergence of metaphor. The process of performance is itself a kind of reading, very much in the sense described by Iser: "an act of defining the oscillating structure of the text through meanings, which as a rule are created in the process of reading itself."[4] This process of definition between dramatic text and audience, a central feature of theatre, makes the reading process here particularly complicated. We might ask, for example, how the concretization of the dramatic text by a reader (in the traditional sense) relates to the concretization by a performance and to the concretization by the audience-reader who witnesses that performance, asking whether performance in fact "fills or rejects" the same gaps as Iser suggests a normal reader does, or whether it fills some and leaves others or creates new ones of its own.

A major concern for the scholar of theatre history is the dynamic involved in the changing interpretations (or readings) of works in different historical periods, a concern of more central interest to Hans Robert Jauss, another pioneer in reception theory. Like Iser, Jauss wishes to emphasize the importance of the reader without giving way to total subjectivism, and for this reason he emphasizes a "specific disposition" of an audience, "which can be empirically determined and which precedes the psychological reaction as well as the subjective understanding of the individual reader."[5] The empirical disposition is provided, according to Jauss, by a "horizon of expectations," itself based upon three factors: "the familiar norms or the immanent poetics of the genre," the "implicit relationships to familiar works of the literary-historical sur-

roundings," and the "opposition between fiction and reality."[6] A number
of useful directions for theatre studies are suggested here, some of which
I will return to presently. Generic expectations and relationships to other
works (intertextuality) are clearly as relevant to theatre reception as to
reading, and the juxtaposition of fiction and reality is perhaps even more
relevant, given the particularly central role played by mimesis and iconicity in the theatre.

Umberto Eco has approached the subject of reader response from a
somewhat different perspective, that of semiotics, and since an important
part of modern theatre studies shares this orientation, it is not surprising
that the theory which has most recently appeared on this subject has had
much closer ties to Eco than to Iser or Jauss. Two of Eco's ideas have
already proved particularly stimulating (though more in general theatre
studies than in studies with a particular historical orientation): that of
the model reader and of open and closed texts. The model reader (a
concept found, in various articulations, in much reading theory) is the
possible reader assumed by the author to whom the book is imaginatively
directed, a reader "supposedly able to deal interpretively with the expressions in the same way as the author deals generatively with them."[7] Any
text, Eco suggests, postulates its own receiver as an indispensable condition of its potential for meaning.

Marco de Marinis, following the lead of Eco, has spoken of the "Model
Spectator," anticipated by theatrical performance.[8] One might, of course,
apply this concept to any historical period, but the modern theatre provides a striking example of the embodiment of this hypothetical construct
in an actual person, the director, who watches the development of a
performance from the seat of a presumed spectator and orchestrates
the effects as such a spectator is expected to receive them. De Marinis
has also applied Eco's distinction of open and closed texts to theatrical
performance, with certain qualifications. Texts that aim at generating a
precise response from a more or less precise group of empirical readers
Eco characterizes as closed, while texts which give fewer and fewer specific response indications are increasingly open.[9] De Marinis suggests
that theatre productions may also tend toward the closed (as in didactic
theatre) or the open (as in much modern avant-garde work), but he also
notes Eco's observation that open works are paradoxically often less accessible than closed ones. Their very lack of specific direction for readers
may restrict their audience to a very few "supercompetent readers" willing to undertake the complex response task put before them. De Marinis
suggests, however, another possibility for open texts in theatre, as in
some traditional Indian performance, where a wide variety of response
is encouraged by an event which attempts to be as inclusive as possible.[10]

Even in "open" texts, the emphasis in Eco remains upon the text as
the primary determinant of the reading situation, and this emphasis is
generally to be found in the more recent work in semiotically oriented

response theory as well. This tendency is not entirely avoided in Iser or Jauss, and Stanley Fish has attempted to avoid such an emphasis by focusing, like Jauss, upon changing interpretations, but more particularly upon the social dynamics by which varying interpretations are advanced and legitimized rather than, like Jauss, upon the mechanisms in the text which permit, or seek to channel, such interpretations. This has led Fish from the "informed reader" of Jauss or the "model reader" of Eco ("informed" and "model" both suggesting authentification by the text) to a "community of readers," socially defined, which shares common values and determines collectively the norms and conventions according to which individual readings will take place. A particularly self-conscious model of such communities may be found in the world of academic criticism in America, where new interpretations are tested against the norms of various reading communities and are given intersubjective validity by the acceptance of these communities. Readings are thus ultimately authenticated not by the text, but by the community.

Fish's approach also provides stimulating possibilities for historical theatre research. The social organization of theatre as created and experienced makes its institutional structure more apparent than that of the book; its communities, by the active choice of assembling to attend plays, are more apparent as groups to themselves and to others than are the more dispersed literary communities. Moreover, one can consider theatre communities on a number of levels, all involved in the formation and authentication of reading strategies, from the rather abstract and scattered communities and subcommunities, which would correspond in the world of theatre to those described by Fish in the literary world, to the specific and unique community assembled for a particular performance.

There is no question that even these unique communities function as a group in the reading process. The social occasion in which theatre is embedded obviously conditions in a major way both the experience and its interpretation. A *New Yorker* cartoon some years ago showed a theatre-audience member, having paused to wipe tears from his cheeks, looking around in some consternation to see that everyone around him was laughing uproariously. "Hey, wait a minute," he says. "Is this satire?" Certainly, in just this way the pressure of audience response can coerce individual members to structure and interpret their experience in a way which might well not have occurred to them as solitary readers and, further, which might not have been within the interpretive boundaries planned by the creators of the performance text.

Theatre history provides many examples of audiences that have not at all responded to a performed work in the expected manner, and the frequency of such disjunctures should provide clear evidence that the community of readers assembled for a theatre event may apply very different strategies from those of the model readers assumed by the performance. Problems are particularly likely to arise when an experimental work resists the reading strategies of an audience expecting something more conventional. In a regular reading situation, a frustrated reader may simply put her book aside and turn to something else. The theatre, as a social event, encourages more active resistance, and not a few demonstrations and even riots have arisen from performances (such as *Hernani* and *Ubu Roi*) failing to play the game according to the rules many in the audience desired. Every actor or director can recall instances when an audience created a meaning for a line or action not at all intended by the producers, and audiences have been known to wrest interpretive control entirely and openly from expected patterns, treating a presumed serious work, for example, as a stimulus to laughter.

Such occasions give particular importance to the efforts of theorists such as Fish to find a theory of reading response which would not ultimately lead back to the text as the basic determinant of meaning. A useful definition of reading provided by Tony Bennett looks in this direction, and I would like to utilize it as the basis for the specific explorations in this area which follow: "the means and mechanisms whereby all texts—literary, filmic, and televisual; fictional or otherwise—may be 'productively activated' during what is traditionally, and inadequately, thought of as the process of their consumption or reception."[11]

When we are dealing not with the sort of recorded texts listed by Bennett but with the text of theatrical performance, what de Marinis has called the "spectacle text," we are really speaking, as has already been noted, of two readings and thus of two simultaneous "productive activations": that of the performance itself and that of the audience. The means and mechanisms by which the first of these readings takes place—that is, the conversion of a literary text into a spectacle text—has of course been given frequent attention in the study of theatre history; but very little attention has been paid to the other reading, the contribution of the audience, and less still to the factors which contribute to the formation of that reading. This is, of course, more closely analogous to what concerns Bennett in the process of reading traditional texts.

Some general indications of how theatre historians might make use of some of the insights of theorists such as Iser, Jauss, Eco, Fish, and Bennett have already been suggested, but it might be helpful to illustrate these procedures with some specific examples. I would like to suggest four historical "means and mechanisms" which have provided audiences with strategies for organizing and interpreting their involvement with the theatre event, some of them closely analogous with means available to readers of written texts, others based upon the particular characteristics of theatre as performance. The first relates directly to Jauss' remarks on the response orientation of the phenomenon of genre, and here we are dealing most closely with the written script. The next, lines of business, looks at a related strategy in the performance itself. The other two are more related to the views of Fish and Bennett, to the work of social institutions, including that of the theatre itself, in the formation or guiding of reading. First we will look briefly at the phenomenon of publicity and programs, then at the effects of institutionalized "readers": dramaturges and reviewers.

Throughout much of the history of Western theatre a strong conservatism in subject matter and genre organization has provided spectators with highly predictable psychic models to apply in the reading of new dramatic pieces (or in revivals of older ones). From Greek until fairly recent times the designation of a play as a comedy or a tragedy alerted the spectator to expect a certain emotional tone, certain types of characters, even certain themes and a certain structure of action.

The Greeks established the practice of taking the plots of their tragedies from familiar stories of legend, myth, and history; and, as Tadeusz Kowzan has pointed out, the drama since classic times has been the literary mode particularly open to reworkings of previously treated character relationships and configurations of action.[12] The spectators who attended the original performances of the classic Greek tragedies attended also a Proagon opening the dramatic festival, during which the authors and actors were introduced and the names of the plays to be performed were announced.[13] Since the general structure of tragedy was given and the stories were drawn from the cultural storehouse, these spectators arrived at the theatre with a good deal of their reading strategy already in place, even when the play had never been presented before. In later times, as the classic works were revived, previous acquaintance with a particular dramatic action added further preparation for audience members. Classic comedy did not, like tragedy, deal with material from history and legend; but by Roman times a remarkably consistent narrative structure involving trickery and love intrigues had been developed for this genre, with an attendant character configuration which reemerged in both the learned and popular comedy of the Renaissance, and which has strongly influenced comedic structure and thus audience anticipation ever since.

Toward the end of the eighteenth century, the traditional firm generic divisions of comedy and tragedy were increasingly attacked, and romantic theorists such as Hugo called in the name of freedom and liberty for the destruction of all rules and traditions which might hinder the free play of artistic imagination.[14] The particular targets of romantic attack—traditional neoclassic comedy and tragedy, already largely exhausted—were in the long run not difficult to overcome, but the idea of genre itself was too central to the dynamic of audience response to be so easily put aside. The popular theatre in particular found, as always, that audiences were more comfortable with plays they could experience in generally predictable ways, and the postromantic theatre, far from freeing itself from the restrictions of genre, developed instead a great variety of more particularized genres, each of which tended to be supported by its own public, familiar with its rules.

The old theatrical monopolies in London and Paris were now no longer in effect, and a large number of theatres competed for a public. Many of these gained and held a public by specializing in certain types of plays, often written especially for those theatres by house dramatists. Thus, even if a nineteenth-century spectator did not know what specific play was being performed at a certain theatre, he or she could predict with reasonable assurance the *type* of play offered there, with all the attendant generic expectations—whether it be a nautical melodrama, a vaudeville, a burletta, a domestic comedy, or a fairy spectacle. Audience participation at that theatre could be expected to be very similar to previous experiences at the same locale.

The public attending such a theatre may be considered as constituting one of Fish's "interpretive communities," parallel in many respects to the literary subcommunities Fish locates in present-day America: "Within the literary community there are subcommunities (what would excite the editors of *Diacritics* is likely to distress the editors of *Studies in Philology*)."[15] Similarly one might say that what would excite nineteenth-century audiences of the London Adelphi or the Bouffes-Parisiens would be likely to distress the audiences of Covent Garden or the Comédie Française.

The high predictability of genre organization in the traditional theatre is very closely related to a high degree of predictability in dramatic characters, and so from genre we move naturally to the practice of lines of business. Researchers into narrative codes such as Propp and Greimas have found certain basic patterns of character relationships and their actantial patterns in many narrative structures, but actantial patterns in theatre, like genre definitions, have throughout much of theatre history been more highly codified and more predictable than those in other narrative traditions. In the *commedia dell'arte,* for example, the traditional comic structure of frustrated young lovers, an elderly blocking agent, and a wily servant was filled by a very specific and highly detailed set of characters, largely unchanged through thousands of performances and generations of audiences. The *commedia* spectator could expect Pantalone, identifiable by mask, costume, and dialect, to be the stubborn father or jealous elderly husband; Il Capitano to be the foolish rival; Harlequin, the clever if mercurial servant; and so on.

Further, the same actors would portray these characters in scenario after scenario, so that audiences could expect certain actions, even certain gestures, from certain actors. This close relationship between actor and specific role or type of role was especially marked in the highly codified theatre of the Renaissance and the early baroque period, but even though some subsequent eras and some actors have emphasized versatility in interpretation, there has never been a period in theatre history without a rather high correlation between specific actors and specific types of roles. We are perhaps most familiar with this custom in connection with the stock roles in nineteenth-century melodrama, but long before the rise of melodrama, actors specialized in noble fathers, male romantic leads, tyrants, soubrettes, and ingenues. Nor is this a peculiarly European phenomenon. The classic Sanskrit theatre manual, the *Natyasastra*, contains lengthy descriptions of a great array of traditional stock character types, and Japanese Kabuki contains carefully delineated traditional role categories. Actors perform in the same categories throughout their lives, and the few who change (such as Ichinatsu Sanokama I in the eighteenth century, who began playing young women and changed to villains in later life) are regarded with some amazement.[16]

There are many reasons for this widespread tendency in theatre. Most basic, surely, is the fact that an actor is always to some extent limited by the appearance and capabilities of his or her own body. In the course of theatre history men have played women and women men, youths played aged and the aged youths, physically unprepossessing actors have created dashing heroes, and magnificent physical specimens hidden their endowments as grotesques and clowns, but there is always a strong tendency pressing actor or actress toward certain roles for which they seem especially suited physically or emotionally. Not surprisingly, there is a high degree of correlation between the ideals of masculine and feminine beauty at different periods and the actors and actresses displayed in the theatre as objects of those periods' desires. One of the earliest extended treatises on the art of acting, Sainte-Albine's *Le Comédien* in 1749, remarked that although many physical types were acceptable on the stage, actors, whatever their abilities, could not depart far from audience expectations for the type of roles they were playing—heroes must have imposing bodies and lovers attractive ones; actors must look the proper age for their roles and have the natural vocal qualities suitable for their characters.[17]

The commercial theatre has always been especially involved with a certain predictability in casting, not only on the grounds of Sainte-Albine's concerns with verisimilitude, but also from a desire to repeat a proven success. If the public has enjoyed a certain actor in a certain role, there has always been strong commercial pressure on him to repeat that character in other plays or to create other characters so similar that the actor can essentially present the same persona. Contemporary television and popular films provide overwhelming evidence of the continuing appeal of this kind of predictable characterization and plotting, and theatre history abounds in instances of audiences bitterly protesting a popular actor's unexpectedly appearing in a role out of harmony with a previously established persona. Clearly, these audiences had come to the theatre with certain strategies already in place for their own contribution to the performance event and were angered by being offered material that resisted the play they were attempting to see.

Since theatre analysis in the past has emphasized the study of the text and of the performance over the study of reception, it has given almost no attention to those elements of the event structure (aside from text and performance or of the larger social milieu) which may be as important to the formation of the reading of the experience as anything actually presented on the stage. To a few such elements—publicity, programs, and reviews—we shall now turn. The neglect so far of such matters by theatre semioticians interested in reading formations is perhaps even more surprising than their neglect by theatre historians, since message-bearing constructs of this sort constitute for most audiences the most obvious first exposure to the possible world of the performance they are going to see. Moreover, these elements are often consciously produced by the institution which also produces the performance as devices for stimulating in particular directions the desires and the interpretive strategies of the spectator.

Theatre programs in the modern sense appeared during the latter part of the nineteenth century, often in a form somewhat suggestive of the printed bill of fare at an elegant dinner. The usual basic form is still widely followed today—the name of the theatre followed by the title and author of the play being presented. Next comes a listing of the characters (often with a brief indication of their relationships) and the actors portraying them, and then information on the time and place of the action. Even this relatively modest body of information provides a certain orientation for the audience and unquestionably affects its reading, as was strikingly illustrated in the recent play *Sleuth,* which achieved part of its surprise effect by providing the audience with false information in the program.

The typical program in the American professional theatre today provides the names of other participating creators, such as costume and lighting designers, and, if the play is a musical, a chronological listing of the songs, which may be considered in part an orienting device for the audience. The most substantial addition to this basic material is normally a brief biography of the participating actors, director, and designers, encouraging a kind of intertextuality peculiar to theatre and film: the remembrance of actors in previous roles.

Programs in many of the American regional and university theatres and in many European countries are far more involved in the process of affecting reading formations. Most obvious are the plot summaries often provided for plays in foreign languages or for plays of particularly difficult or complex action (Shakespearian history plays, for example, which may even include genealogical tables in the programs). The plot summaries provided by Peter Sellars for his highly innovative interpretations of traditional operatic works often are more iconoclastic than anything he places on stage and clearly are created to prepare the audience, violently if necessary, for his new readings of familiar texts. Interpretive essays by a director or dramaturg often seek to condition audience response in an even more programmatic way, and such conditioning need not even take the form of discursive analysis. Programs often include sketches, literary quotations, or photographs not directly related to the play, but suggesting a preferred interpretive strategy. Even a single image can have a profound effect upon interpretation. Consider the differences in reading encouraged in two audiences attending Shakespeare's *Henry V*, one given a program whose cover depicts a British flag or a soldier in heroic pose, sword uplifted, and another given a program depicting a broken corpse on the field of battle.

Many modern productions use a specific image or logo not only on the program but also, more important, on posters and in newspaper advertising, so that an audience member's first important impression of the production may well arise from this source. When the theatre production is offered as a commercial product, the logo clearly bears an institutional relationship to commercial symbols used in the advertising of many contemporary products, although most theatre logos avoid the abstract geometrical designs and calligraphic fancies favored for many products by corporations today. Their logos, like the theatre itself, are primarily iconic and are often drawn from a particular visual image within the production, thus foregrounding that image when the production is experienced (the masked figure in *Amadeus*, for example, or the tableau of the prostrate nuns in the Metropolitan Opera's *Dialogues of the Carmelites*).

The use of the logo is one example of how publicity, primarily designed to attract an audience to a specific production, inevitably also affects the reception of that production. Even the composition of the community of readers who make up the theatre audience is closely related to the institutional organization of publicity, since modern audiences, faced with a bewildering selection of possible activities, are extremely dependent upon publicity in order to discover what these alternatives are and to select among them. Well aware of this dynamic, theatres attempt to conceive and to distribute their publicity so that it will be most effective in reaching the audience considered most likely to support this particular production. The response-theory concept of the "model reader" or "implied reader" has particular relevance here, since before that reader enters the theatre or even buys a ticket, he must be targeted and sought by appropriate publicity. Thus, large musicals seeking a mass audience from an entire region may purchase spots on television, while small theatres seeking to develop a local audience will rely upon notices in supermarkets, banks, laundromats, and neighborhood newspapers. In New York the two major outlets for theatrical newspaper advertising are *The New York Times* and the *Village Voice*, associated with reading communities so different that the same production will rarely advertise in both papers. Obviously, larger Broadway productions will advertise in the *Times,* but so will productions (especially musical) which would normally be classified as Off-Broadway but which seek the patronage of an uptown audience. Experimental productions of more limited and specialized appeal seek their audiences in the more congenial *Voice.*

The two invariable elements of the newspaper advertisement (and of its eighteenth- and nineteenth-century predecessor, the playbill) are the essential name of the production and its location. What other elements are included inevitably provide information about the desired self-image of the production and thus, like the logo, provide anticipatory suggestions for the public's reading strategies. English playbills of the late eighteenth century normally included only the names of the playhouse, the play, and the actors and their roles. In the course of the nineteenth century, when many productions were created whose major focus was visual spectacle, this orientation was reflected on playbills which listed the sequence of scenic effects, often devoting to them more space and a more impressive typeface than that given to the actors. An 1870 playbill from the Queen's Theatre, Longacre, for *A Midsummer Night's Dream* leaves little doubt as to how this particular performance is intended to be read. Immediately under the title of the play comes the name of the scenic designer, then the props master, then the designers of machinery and costumes, then the choreographer and conductor, then the actors. Next, occupying the largest and most ornate section of the playbill, comes a scene-by-scene listing of visual effects. The first three scenes will give an idea of the whole:

Act 1, scene 1. PERISTYLE OF THESEUS' PALACE, OVERLOOKING ATHENS. Scene 2. QUINCE, the Joiner's Workshop, COPIED FROM THE DISCOVERIES OF HERCULENEUM. Act 2, scene 1. A WOOD NEAR ATHENS! MEETING OF OBERON AND TITANIA, AND 150 ELVES AND FAIRIES.

Obviously advertising of this sort, especially for productions of Shakespeare, disappeared with the disappearance of scenically oriented revivals in the early twentieth century, but advertising today will still suggest when some element in the production apparatus is being foregrounded, such as the director ("The Peter Brook production of A MIDSUMMER NIGHT'S DREAM,") or a leading actor ("the RSC presents Anthony Sher in RICHARD III").

So important has advance publicity become in the modern theatre, and so remote is it institutionally from most of those involved in the creation of the production itself, that there is often a danger that the community of readers, or the horizons of expectation of one, may be quite different from that assumed by the other, resulting in serious reading difficulties during the performance. Alan Schneider considered the audience's determination to see a different play than the one he was presenting the paramount reason for the disastrous American premiere of *Waiting for Godot* in Miami, and clearly, advance publicity made an important contribution to this. "The Miami audience," reports Schneider, "was being informed, in large type, that Bert Lahr, 'Star of *Harvey* and *Burlesque*,' and Tom Ewell, 'Star of *The Seven-Year Itch*,' were about to appear in their midst in 'The Laugh *Sensation* of Two Continents,' *Waiting for Godot*. The name of the author appeared only in very small print. My name, luckily, hardly appeared at all."

The result was a memorable example of an audience's frustration at attempting to create a particular, expected theatre experience out of extremely recalcitrant material:

> Instead of *The Seven-Year Itch* or *Harvey*, the audience got *Waiting for Godot*, not the "laugh sensation of two continents," but a very strange sensation indeed. At first they laughed—at Bert trying to take off his shoe, at Tommy realizing his fly was unbuttoned; but as soon as they realized that the actors were on to more serious matters, they stopped. By the time they got to the Bible and the Thieves, they were laughless. . . . Whole groups started to sneak out. Then droves. . . . [18]

Fifteen years later in an off-Broadway theatre in New York, with audiences aware that the author of this unconventional play was a major experimental writer and winner of the Nobel prize, and prepared by publicity calling the work not a "laugh sensation" but "a cornerstone of the modern theatre" and "a timeless classic," the play, directed again by Schneider, received a warm and enthusiastic welcome.

This sort of radical disjuncture between the horizon of expectations assumed by the production and that actually brought to the theatre by a community of readers may be encouraged, as it clearly was in Miami, by an institutional disjuncture between publicity and production, but larger structural concerns lie behind this specific manifestation. Toward the end of the eighteenth century and at the beginning of the nineteenth a number of major changes, artistic and political, significantly altered both the creation and staging of plays and the audiences attending them. Out of this crisis emerged a new figure in the theatre, the dramaturg, along with his near relative, the reviewer. Their function was in general to mediate between performance and spectator, suggesting to the latter possible strategies and mechanisms to be employed in reading performances. Like modern publicity, they have often been able to influence reading to such an important extent as to outweigh or even to negate the reading guides of the performance itself.

Although their relationship to reading formations has historically been very similar, the dramaturg and the reviewer come to this function from opposite directions—one from the theatre, the other from the audience. The position of dramaturg is usually considered to have begun in the theatre with the appointment of Gotthold Lessing to this position in Hamburg in 1767. The Hamburg theatre was the first attempt at establishing a German national theatre, and its founders realized that it would not be enough to create an original German repertoire, establish a state-supported cultural institution, and elevate the public image of both stage and actors, difficult as all these tasks were, unless they could at the same time develop an audience, not yet in existence, that could actively and intelligently participate in this new venture. Thus an important element in those essays Lessing wrote for Hamburg was the guiding and developing of proper response skills in the new audience.

The first modern reviews appeared in France somewhat later, but in response to a similar need. Here, the Revolution separated the post-1800 tradition from its roots and its earlier audiences even more radically than had the search for a new literary drama in eighteenth-century Germany. The community of readers which for generations had supported the theatre in France disappeared with the Revolution, and the community which appeared subsequently, eager to participate in the cultural life of novels and theatre, often lacked the knowledge of how to do so. Thus a new community of readers had to be trained.

In response to this need appeared the first modern reviews, the *feuilletons* of Geoffroy in the *Journal des débats*, beginning in 1800. The previous century had seen journalistic reports on the theatre, but these were directed toward a public already familiar with the conventions of the traditional system. Geoffroy's public required from him something quite different: a guide not only to meaningful participation in the theatre event but, perhaps equally important, to subsequent intelligent discussions of that event in the drawing rooms and salons of polite society.[19] For this public, Geoffroy provided much of the sort of material brought to the theatre in earlier times by the audience themselves—intertextual relationships with other works; an acquaintance with the tradition, the author, the actors. He took upon himself the role of model reader and unquestionably was powerfully influential in the training of responses of a whole generation of theatregoers in Paris.

After Geoffroy, the reviewer became a regular feature of the French theatre world, as influential in theatre life as any actor, director, or playwright. The popular impression today of a reviewer is that of a journal writer who advises audiences whether they should attend a play or not, and certainly this function has been a powerful one, especially when such reviews are widely read or quoted and major financial and artistic ventures are at stake. Equally important for the functioning of the theatre, however, is a less generally acknowledged function: the providing of audiences with strategies for the reading of performances. In countries such as America, where dramaturgs related to specific companies are rare, it is often the case that the comments of reviewers, especially regarding unusual or experimental works, are more powerful than any other single source in structuring the way that audiences will receive the performance within the theatre.

Reviewers still commonly follow the example of Geoffroy not only in providing judgments on productions, but also in making intertextual connections, suggesting interpretations, ordering elements, and proposing relationships and emphases by citing particular passages as especially effective or ineffective. An excellent and by no means unusual example of this dynamic at work may be seen in Walter Kerr's review of the highly innovative 1977 production by Andrei Serban of *The Cherry Orchard.* The review begins with a powerful and specific claim for a certain reading of the production: "There are at least five images I shan't forget as long as I live in Andrei Serban's mounting of 'The Cherry Orchard.' . . . " A large part of the remaining rather lengthy article is devoted to a vivid and evocative description of each of these five images, complete in each case with an interpretation. The review then continues with other reading aids, such as this guide to certain relevant intertextuality: " . . . some of these instances have the smell of the circus about them, some of vaudeville, some of chamber music, some of a thumping brass band, some of Peter Brook, and some of Robert Wilson, and some of Samuel Beckett, transformed into a high-wire mountebank. . . . "[20]

So striking and specific a review could hardly fail to condition the subsequent reception of this play by any spectator, and the position of the review, on the front page of the "Arts and Leisure" section of the Sunday *New York Times,* guaranteed that it would be noticed by an important percentage of the production's likely public. For many viewers this review surely provided an important structuring framework ("Ah, here is the third unforgettable image—thus there are still two to come"), and as a member of that public, I can testify that the review foregrounded those images for me in a manner that I found both troublesome and inescapable.

The contribution of reviews to reading formations is reinforced in the modern theatre by the frequent recycling of reviews by the theatre institutions themselves. In the absence of dramaturgs, particularly in the American theatre, both theatre organizations and public have come to accept reviewers as "official" readers of productions, giving to their reactions a particular authority. Short citations from reviews, selected for their presumed ability to stimulate audience interest, have become an almost invariable component of newspaper advertisements and in New York are often also displayed on special signboards at the entrance to the theatre. The frequent hyperbole of such phrases and the fact that they are necessarily taken out of context obviously erodes their authority to some extent but does not remove their power to condition reception. Even a reader who does not believe that a new play is likely to truly be "the wittiest comedy since Noel Coward" will be unlikely, having read such a comment, to see the play without Coward's becoming a more or less conscious intertextual element in the reception.

More detailed and more specific guidance is given when theatres display on their premises entire reviews or newspaper stories, to be read by prospective patrons or, even more significant, by those actually attending the performance. The lobbies of many theatres in London, Paris, and New York today regularly display such reviews, and they are invariably eagerly read by patrons before and after the performance, and, perhaps most important, during the intermissions. The on-site availability of such authorized readings displayed but not created by the organization producing the performance itself provides a contribution to reading formation highly unusual in the history of the theatre, one which would surely repay closer study.

The comparatively small amount of reception research carried out in the theatre to date has been developed almost entirely through interviews and questionnaires seeking to establish what an audience thought or felt about a performance after its completion. Almost no organized work has been done on the other end of this process: what an audience brings to the theatre in the way of expectations, assumptions, and strategies which will creatively interact with the stimuli of the theatre event to produce whatever effect the performance has on this audience and what effect they have upon it. This essay has attempted to suggest, at least in brief form, some of the kinds of material available for such research and how it might be pursued. A clearer understanding of how spectators today and in other historical periods have learned and applied the rules of the game they play with the performance event in the theatre will surely provide us with a far richer and more interesting picture of that complex event than has the traditional model, which treated the spectator as essentially a passive recipient of the stage's projected stimuli.

NOTES

1. The work that has appeared has been largely semiotic in orientation and so far has dealt very little with specifically historical questions. A leading representative of this approach is Marco de Marinis, most recently in "Dramaturgy of the Spectator," *TDR* 31, 2 (Summer 1987), 100–14, and earlier in "L'esperienza dello spettatore: fondamenti per una semiotica della ricezione teatrale," *Documenti di lavoro* 138–39 (1984), Centro di Semiotica e Linguistica di Urbino, and "Theatrical Comprehension: A Socio-Semiotic Approach," *Theater* 15, 1 (Winter 1983), 8–15. A special issue of *VS*, no. 41 (May–Aug. 1985), was devoted to "Semiotica della ricezione teatrale." See also Darko Suvin, "The Performance Text as Audience-Stage Dialog Inducing a Possible World," *VS*, 42 (Sept.–Oct. 1985), 3–20.

2. Wolfgang Iser, *Die Appellstruktur der Texte* (Konstanz, 1970), 15.

3. Anne Ubersfeld, *Lire le théâtre* (Paris, 1977), 24.

4. Iser, *Appellstruktur*, 11.

5. Hans Robert Jauss, *Toward an Aesthetic of Reception*, trans. Timothy Bahti (Minneapolis, 1982), 22–23.

6. Jauss, *Aesthetic*, 25.

7. Umberto Eco, *The Role of the Reader* (Bloomington, 1979), 7.

8. Marco de Marinis, *Semiotica del teatro* (Milan, 1982), 198–99, and "Dramaturgy," 102–3.

9. Eco, *Role*, 7–8.

10. De Marinis, "Dramaturgy," 103–4.

11. Tony Bennett, "Text, Readers, Reading Formations," *Literature and History*, 9 (1983), 214.

12. Tadeusz Kowzan, *Littérature et spectacle dans leurs rapports esthétiques, thématiques, et sémiologiques* (Warsaw, 1975), 25.

13. Arthur Pickard-Cambridge, *The Dramatic Festivals of Athens* (Oxford, 1968), 67.

14. Perhaps most famous is the preface to *Cromwell*, which called for "the liberty of art against the despotism of systems, codes, and rules." Victor Hugo, *Oeuvres complètes*, 18 vol. (Paris, 1967), 3:77.

15. Stanley Fish, *Is There a Text in this Class?* (Cambridge, 1980), 349.

16. Earle Ernst, *The Kabuki Theatre* (New York, 1956), 200.

17. Pierre Rémond de Sainte-Albine, *Le Comédien* (Paris, 1749), 228.

18. Alan Schneider, *Entrances* (New York, 1986), 232.

19. Charles Marc des Granges, *Geoffroy et la critique dramatique* (Paris, 1897), 120–21.

20. Walter Kerr, *New York Times*, Sunday, Feb. 27, 1977, II, 1, 5. This sort of authoritative reading may be seen in film reviewing as well. A recent review by David Denby (*New York*, June 22, 1987, 71) begins: "There are exactly two good scenes in *The Witches of Eastwick*."

✳ ✳ ✳ ✳ ✳   The Semiotics of
Character Names in the
Drama

Julian: You . . . you *are* the butler, are you not,
        but . . .
Butler: Butler. My name is Butler.
Julian: How extraordinary!
Butler: No, not really. Appropriate.
        Bulter . . . butler. If my name were
        Carpenter, and I were a butler . . . or if
        I *were* a carpenter and my name were
        Butler . . .
Julian: But still . . .
Butler: . . . it would not be so appropriate.
                                    Edward Albee, *Tiny Alice*

IN THE HIGHLY CONCENTRATED narrative world of the drama, the names
given to characters potentially provide a powerful communicative device
for the dramatist seeking to orient his audience as quickly as possible in
his fictive world. Thus from the very beginnings of drama we may see
working a variety of onomastic codes, differing from era to era, but
always an important part of the general semiotic system of theatre.
Through these codes audiences have traditionally been provided with
information not only about the character who bears a particular name,
but also about his actantial role in a total dramatic structure, about his
place in a pattern of relationships, and about intertextual relations between the drama in which he appears and other dramas of the same or
of contrasting genres. The names of characters provided one of the codes
that contrasted comedy and tragedy in classic Greece. Tragedy writers,
Aristotle observed, used real or historical names, while the writers of
comedy used fictitious ones. Commentators on Aristotle have never

agreed upon his exact idea of comic names, some interpreting him to mean that these names are selected essentially by chance, others that they are selected with a clear signifying function in mind. Thus the Bywater translation says that the comic poets use "any names that may occur to them" while Butcher says they use "characteristic names." There is some evidence to support each reading,[1] and I will presently consider both approaches to naming, but all interpreters agree that the Greek dramatists did employ contrasting naming codes, with comedy relying in general upon found or invented names, and tragedy upon names drawn from history or mythology.

If we follow the interpretation of Bywater and others, taking comedy names as chosen essentially at random, we may use a term sometimes employed by these critics: "chance" names. One may regard such names, or such a naming strategy, as one end of a spectrum of onomastic codes used at various times by the theatre. If the bearers of "chance" names are, in a sense, not "bound" to their names, the opposite end of the spectrum would be represented by a code in which the characters and names are identical, as in the morality play. Morality characters *are* their names. The names are definitive and totally encompassing; no extra-nominal "residue" extends beyond them. Between these two extremes it is possible to trace a series of other fairly distinct naming conventions, each employing a different mode of signification and each associated with particular genres and particular periods of the drama. And each, of course, provides for its own audience important information for the "reading" of the dramatic structure as a whole.

Only a small number of plays employ the most extreme form of a "chance" name, one totally free of the created character and thus beyond any selective process, conscious or unconscious, of the author. Pirandello's *Tonight We Improvise*, some of the recent *Mitspiele* of Paul Pörtner, and other modern experimental works have offered characters created without names who are to assume the names of the actors portraying them. While this is not a common theatrical code, audiences, at least in recent times, accustomed to experiments in blending reality and illusion in the theatre, seem to have little difficulty in "reading" in such a code an attempt at a greater conflation of actor and character than is sought in traditional theatre.

"Chance" names selected by the dramatist are, of course, much more common phenomena. This approach, with some important qualifications that we shall presently consider, is particularly closely tied with realistic and naturalistic drama, the dominant form of the past century. As a part of its attempt to create the impression of a "slice of life," such theatre naturally employs as many as possible of the codes of everyday social action—codes of language, of gesture, of costume, and so on. The audience is encouraged to consider these codes, even when adjusted for theatrical purposes, as essentially identical to their extratheatre parallels, and to "read" them as they would outside the theatre. The naming of characters in such drama tends to follow this overall pattern. The more closely a dramatist adheres to the "slice-of-life" ideal, the closer his names will be to "chance" names.

Even this close to the "natural" end of the spectrum, however, the term "chance" can be misleading. The realistic dramatist's goal, after all, is to create not a world of random particles, but a world organized apparently like our own. Far from chosing names at random, the realistic dramatist must be closely aware of the naming codes operating in the society his drama seeks to mirror. A name truly chosen at random would run almost as much risk of calling unwanted attention to the theatrical artifice as a name obviously selected for its theatrical effect. Perhaps the most basic of all the naming codes of society is that of sexual differentiation. Strindberg's *Comrades* is a rare example of a realistic drama that contradicts social codes in this respect, providing "male" names for certain female characters, but the effect sought is precisely the arousal in the audience of a feeling of tension and uneasiness that the breaking of this same code would cause in the external world.

National, regional, and ethnic names are probably the next most general type of coding, and here, too, the realistic dramatist must attend not only to popular usage but also to the semantic overtones often attached to both given and family names of this type. O'Neill's Ephraim Cabot is as solidly attached to New England as Hansberry's Travis Younger is to the black South. The ethnic conflicts—Italian, Jewish, and WASP—in Innaurato's *Gemini* are clearly reflected in the names—Fran and Francis Geminiani, Bunny and Herschel Weinberger, Judith and Randy Hastings. For so-called ethnic and regional dramatists such names provide an important part of the embedding of the drama in its appropriate milieu, but any realistic play is ethnic and regional to some degree, and the names employed almost invariably help to locate its fictive world.

Related to the ethnicity and regionality of names is the social position they imply. Certain names or types of names in every society seem more "proper" for the leaders of society and others for those near the bottom of the social ladder. In European drama names frequently reflect long-established class structures, while in America there is a high correlation between status of names and waves of immigration, with British names ranking generally highest (rivaled perhaps by French names in the South), other northern European names less high, Irish lower, and eastern European and Mediterranean lower still. A memorable confrontation of names with a heavy weight of ethnic and social connotations occurs in *A Streetcar Named Desire*, pitting the faded aristocratic elegance of Blanche Dubois against the crude vitality of Stanley Kowalski.

As these examples suggest, both given and family names may suggest not only social roles, but character qualities. Clearly Williams seeks to suggest a delicate, even ethereal quality in his hapless heroines by the use of such names as Blanche, Amanda, and Alma (which, as she herself is fond of observing, is Spanish for soul). Changing fashions in names require that the realistic dramatist be sensitive to the associations of names within his own society. Names like Luke and Ned, Flora and Flossie, quite acceptable for heroes and heroines of the nineteenth century, have an antiquated and rural feeling today. Once-elegant male names like Percival, Marmaduke, or Sebastian now suggest comic affectation, effeminacy, or even decadence.

The comments and practice of the leading naturalist dramatists have from the beginning confirmed that in fact careful attention was given by them to the selection of names. Zola called this selection a "science," and observed that he would "often spend days together over a Paris Directory, making out a list of names which strike me as valuable and likely to be useful, and a much longer time in finally selecting out of a list derived from that source the one or two that I may be in want of." He characterized himself as a "fatalist in the matter of names, believing firmly that a mysterious correlation exists between the man and the name he bears."[2] The surviving draft versions of Ibsen's plays show a similar concern, Ibsen often trying a whole series of names before finding the one he considered appropriate to the evolving character.

The historical drama, like the drama of realism, looks to the world outside the theatre for its naming codes, but the rules governing the selection of names in such plays are in fact quite different. Aristotle suggests that the writers of tragedy begin with certain patterns of action and then seek the proper sequence of events and patterns of relationships in history that fit these. His analysis has been disputed, but it does call attention to the structural quality of historical material. Historical names come already imbued with accompanying actions and embedded in a constellation of other names, related to one another in an established actantial pattern. Thus the use of Orestes implies that of Clytemnestra, Agamemnon, and Electra; the use of Mary Stuart, that of Elizabeth, Leicester, and Burleigh; the use of Joan of Arc, that of Charles and Dunois.

With such familiar names and relationships a dramatist can rarely depart far from the historical encoding already accepted by his potential audience. With less prominent characters more freedom is possible, but a somewhat different constraint appears. Here historical accuracy, or to be more exact, faithfulness to the accepted tradition is of little concern compared with the necessity of making the selected names seem geographically and temporally appropriate for the hypothetical historical world being created. Shakespeare, Schiller, and Strindberg generally drew names for secondary characters directly from the historical chronicles serving as their sources, even when they were not scrupulously accurate about the historical roles played by these names. Studies of Racine and his sources have demonstrated that to fill in the secondary characters around his more familiar classic heroes and heroines Racine referred to an extensive collection of Greco-Roman sources for names with the proper sound and classic feeling.[3]

During certain periods there has been a vogue for historical drama of another type, not based upon well-known or at least somewhat-known characters from national history or from classic history and myth, but depicting characters, events, and settings far removed from the experience and knowledge of the spectators. Many English heroic tragedies of the Restoration are of this type, as are the Turkish and Oriental dramas that enjoyed a vogue in France during the seventeenth century or certain exotic spectacle dramas of the romantic period. Our first impression of the names in such plays is that they bear a much more simple and direct message than that carried by the names just discussed— that their major, if not sole, function is to support the scenery and costume in signaling to the spectator an alien and exotic society. Clearly this is of central importance, but when we examine specific uses of such names we almost invariably find that they bear much more information than simple exoticism.

In the nineteenth century, when historicism and historical research were much in vogue, it is hardly surprising to find that dramatists tended to devote the same care to researching correct names for characters in a drama set in postclassic Athens, preconquest Peru, or medieval Byzantium as for those in the more familiar historical events of their own nations. Audiences of this period expected such dramas to be educative as well as exotic, and dramatists such as Pixérécourt and Sardou devoted great attention to historical research in order to defend themselves, as both had to do, against scholarly criticism on the accuracy of historical detail in even the most remote and obscure settings.

One might expect dramatists of the seventeenth and eighteenth centuries to be much more casual in the creation of names for such dramas, but in fact they display a similar respect for historical sources. Probably the pattern already set of researching suitable classic names for neoclassic dramas carried over into dramas with other settings, but doubtless equally important was the tradition, dating back to the Greeks, of creating new plays, especially serious ones, by reworking earlier stories rather than by creating new ones. A drama drawn from an Oriental or Arabic source would come already furnished with suitable names, and when other characters needed to be added, the dramatist tended to go to related sources for them rather than attempt to coin new ones. Moreover, we must realize that many dramatic names from this period that seem quite bizarre and arbitrary to our contemporary consciousness in fact evoked a familiar fictive world to audiences of earlier periods. A good example of this is the Moorish names of the Abencerrages and the Zegrys in Dryden's *Conquest of Granada*—Abdelmelech, Zulema, Lyndaraxa, Benzayda, and so on. Today these are likely to be read essentially as alien constellations of sounds, but for much of Dryden's own audience they evoked not only a particular historical and geographic context, but moreover a specific literary tradition.

Pérez de Hita's *Historia de las Guerras Civiles de Granada*, the basic source for these names and for the actions in which they were involved, had not yet been translated into English, but it and other Spanish histories were well known in England in their original language.[4] Even more important, the *Historia*, first published in 1606, had been translated into French in 1608 and had since that time served as the inspiration for a whole series of plays and novels, including, in the years just before Dryden's play, *Almahide*, by the popular Mme de Scudéry. Mme de La Fayette's *Zaide*, employing the same names, appeared contemporaneously with *The Conquest of Granada*. Thus for Dryden and most of his public these names, though exotic, were familiar and accessible literary references.

It is important to stress, however, that an audience brings to names of this sort a literary rather than a historical consciousness, even though the names, technically speaking, are historical. What this means is that with such names we are a step further removed from the "chance" or "found" names of naturalism. The names of history, while more remote than the names of naturalistic drama, still called upon the audience to read them in the light of codes brought from outside the art. Dryden's Moors began to look more toward a fictive code, and thus point away from the drama of realism to that of convention and artistic self-consciousness. From this point on, there tends to be a sharp distinction between names found on stage and those found in life. The author no longer seeks to hide all traces of his manipulation, but assigns names that the audience at once may recognize as signals for a specific reading of the theatrical artifact.

Certain "fictive" names operate in a manner analogous to historical names—that is, they may be used in a variety of plays by different authors, even of different historical periods, while maintaining along with their names certain sets of actions or certain personality traits. Indeed, one may trace a range of dramatic possibilities from outright historical figures, such as one finds in the German docudramas of the 1960s, through the somewhat fictionalized figures of Lincoln or Joan of Arc, on to figures like Faust or Don Juan, where the historical originals have virtually disappeared, at last to figures like Sherlock Holmes, entirely fictive, but distinct enough as individuals to contribute centrally to establishing a fictive universe in any dramatic structure where they appear. Some such figures last for centuries, but almost every period also offers fictive names that are used for a series of plays by one or several authors and then disappear, like Madame Angot in Napoleonic France or Robert Macaire during the French Restoration.

Such names bring with them a high degree of individualization and frequently elements of a plot structure as well. Less detailed and specific, but no less individualized, are the stock names of many theatre traditions, the most famous being those of the *commedia dell'arte*, such as Harlequin, Pantalone, or Pulcinella. For centuries names like these brought with them a whole theatrical gestalt, including a certain mask and costume, posture and gestures, personality and habits, as well as standardized and predictable relationships with other members of the same dramatic structure. In addition to these best-known names, there were hundreds of other traditional names in the *commedia* tradition, some specific to a single country, some popular only for a generation or two, some associated with a single actor, but each utilized in a number of different plays and bringing to each new play a set of interrelated physical and costumic signs that the audience was expected to understand as part of the code system of that performance.

Doubtless this *commedia* practice contributed to the common employment in the seventeenth- and eighteenth-century French theatre of certain stock names in all dramatic genres, many of them Greek or Italianized pseudo-Greek. Such names were not only, as in the *commedia*, associated with certain characters—fathers, servants, young lovers, and so on—but also with certain genres: Tircis and Philis with pastorals; Orgon, Orante, Géronte, Dorante with comedy; Attale, Nérine, Olympe, Cléone with tragedy. Thus the use of such a name indicated at once to a spectator not only a type of character but a type of dramatic structure, since each genre followed fairly predictable patterns of plot with fairly predictable configurations of actants. Dramatic companies, like *commedia* companies, were organized so that each actor regularly assumed a certain type of role and therefore might appear in a number of plays not only as the same general character, but with the same name. Herzel has traced this process in Molière's troupe. The comic servant Sganarelle always belonged to Molière. La Grange played young lovers—Dorante, Cléonte, Valère—Mlle de Brie the objects of their affection—Mariane, Elise—and Mlle Béjart the sprightly maids—Lisette, Dorine.[5] When the curtain first rose on Molière's *The Miser*, revealing the popular actors La Grange and Mlle de Brie, the original audience could assume before a word was spoken that these were the young lovers whose temporary frustration and eventual bliss would be a central concern of the action. When these actors at once identified each other as Valère and Elise, this removed any possible remaining doubts on the matter.

Austin has shown this association of certain names with certain types of character to be at work in Roman comedy, as, for example, in the slave names of Terence, where in several plays Syrus is a crafty and a potentially treacherous rogue, somewhat akin to the *commedia* figure. Brighella, Daros, and Geta are also crafty but loyal to their masters; Parmeno is trustworthy, but stolid and unimaginative, while Dromio is so dull and slow that he is fit only for the most menial work. There is some evidence that other Roman comedy authors used these same names for similar characters.

Names like Orgon and Dorante, while immediately recognizable to a French spectator of the seventeenth or eighteenth century as belonging to a character of a certain type and age, had little specific etymological significance. At the next stage of theatricalization we find names, especially within the comedic tradition, that carry within themselves a more obviously artificial and specific message about their bearer. These may be designated as "speaking" names, one of the most popular and obvious onomastic devices used by the drama. Such names traditionally do not pass on from play to play in the manner of the stock names just considered, though certain types of "speaking" names work in a manner very similar to stock names, indicating a consistent type filling a predictable actantial role in the dramatic structure. The most famous example, as well as the most durable, is the braggart soldiers of Roman comedy, whose signifying names vary widely, but are all related by their pompous exaggeration and reveling in death and destruction.

Plautus sets the style with such examples as Pyrgopolynices (taker of towers) and Polymachaeroplagides (son of many blows of the dagger), and during the sixteenth and seventeenth centuries such figures appeared across Europe—in Italy, Capitano Spaveto della Valle Inferna (Fearsome of Hell's Valley), Capitano Spaccamonti (Mountain-splitter), and Capitano Spezzaferro (Iron-breaker); from France, Engoulevent (Swallower-up) and Fracasso-brise-tout (Fracasso-break-all); from Spain, Sangre y Fuego (Blood and fire); from Germany, Horribilifax; and from England, Ralph Roister Doister, Roughman, and Rakehell. The later Restoration fop is another such type of character, whose actantial role remains much the same whether his "speaking" name is Sir Fopling Flutter, Lord Foppington, or Sir Novelty Fashion.

When such speaking names are given to characters appearing in essentially the same configuration in a whole series of plays, they reveal a system analogous to that of the *commedia* or of the stock naming system of classic French comedy. A good example of this is the nautical melodrama of the nineteenth-century British theatre, where the hero is given some such patriotic, determined, or gear-and-tackle name as Will Steady, Harry Hallyard, Jack Gallant, Jack Stedfast, Harry Bowline, or Union Jack. The villain, in contrast, bears a dark, foreign, or aristocratic name: Sir William Pledger, Black Ralph, Black Brandon, or Mordenbrenner. The heroine is normally given a romantic, faintly Italianate name, usually without a "speaking" function, while the comic man and comic woman's names will "speak" in a somewhat precious or ridiculous manner, as in Becky Butterfly or Sampson Sawdust. As in Molière's theatre, this naming system was reinforced by the fact that each actor in a company specialized in certain types of roles and therefore assumed certain types of names. Thomas B. Cooke, for example, made a career of the steadfast-British-sailor roles.

"Speaking" names vary widely, but most fall into one of four general types, the first three normally given to lesser characters in the dramatic action and the fourth to both major and minor characters. First there are animal names, usually suggesting character traits but sometimes profession. The most famous set of these occurs in Jonson's *Volpone*, where all the intriguers have Italianate animal names and only the two innocent young people, Celia and Bonairo, are given more normal, but still significant names, suggesting heaven and goodness. Jonson's *Epicoene* includes a "land and sea captain" named Tom Otter, and another sea captain in *Eastward Ho* is called Seagull. Farquhar's *Recruiting Officer* has a "country clown" named Bullock, and a duplicitous tale-bearer in *School for Scandal* is call Snake. Feydeau used this device from time to time, as in naming a bashful young suitor de Vaux (calf).

A second type of such name derives from objects, almost always associated with the character's trade. Farquhar names his recruiting officer Captain Plume, two justices Mr. Balance and Mr. Scale, and a highwayman Gibbet. Vanbrugh's *Relapse* has a surgeon called Syringe, and Massinger's *A New Way to Pay Old Debts* has an alehouse keeper and his wife named Tapwell and Froth. Nestroy uses many such names—Zech (bill) for a waiter, Aspic for a cook, Zris (rent) for a landlord, Fingerhut (thimble) for a tailor, Fett (lard) for a butcher. The cooks in Plautus's *Mostellaria* are called Anthrax (coal) and Macherio (knife), while the parasite Peniculus (little brush) in the *Menaechmi* is so called, as he himself remarks in the play, because he sweeps the table clean.

A third category looks not at the objects of a character's trade, but at the trade's actions. So we find Vanbrugh's Coupler, a matchmaker, or Treble, a singing master; Farquhar's Tom Errand, a porter; Shirley's barber Master Haircut and procuress Madame Decoy; and Splitgut, the butcher's apprentice in *Eastward Ho*. The medieval French *Jeu de Saint Nicolas* gives "speaking" names to a band of rogues: Cliquet (jabberer), Pincedé (dice-pincher), and Rasoir (sharper). One of the striking features of the codes that structure "speaking" names related to trades and professions is that while such names may derive from tools or actions, the most obvious signifying names, denoting the professions themselves, are not used in this context, probably because such names are often in fact encountered in real life, as in the English Cook, Farmer, and Tailor, or their German equivalents, Kock, Meier, and Schneider. Such names thus lack the artificiality and therefore the humor and artistic self-consciousness of the sort of names that are used. The single exception to this rule in my acquaintance occurs in Albee's *Tiny Alice*, a quotation from which prefaces this essay, but the device here is used less for comic codification than as one among many devices in this particular play (such as cardinals in the Cardinal's garden) to create a kind of hall of mirrors.

Certain names in this third category begin to overlap with the fourth and largest, where the emphasis is less upon profession than upon character description. A few such names are so obvious as to suggest morality figures, such as Mr. Jolly and Mr. Sadd in Killigrew's *The Parson's Wedding*, but the majority are more sophisticated, generally being composed of an adjective-noun, verb-noun, adverb-noun, or verb-adverb combination. Most of the braggart soldiers already mentioned fall into this category. Scattered examples may be found in the English medieval drama. The Wakefield cycle, for example, offers a shepherd named Slow-Pace, a messenger in *Caesar Augustus* named Lightfoot, and a torturer in *The Talents* named Spell Pain. Coding of this type was a standard feature of English comedy from the Renaissance through the early nineteenth century, when plays abounded with characters such as Mr. Bearjest, Lady Lovewell, Lord Morelove, Lady Graveairs, Pinchwife, Lady Lurewell, and Lady Sneerwell. Adding a first name often allows the addition of another descriptive adjective, as in Pecunious Lucre, Sir Feeble Fainwould, Sir Cautious Fulbank, or Sir Tunbelly Clumsy.

That the same practice may be found in Germanic comedy of the same period is supported by the critical authority of Lessing, who devoted two numbers (90 and 91) of his *Hamburgische Dramaturgie* to the matter of names in drama, observing that comedy traditionally

> gave names to its personages, names which by means of the grammatical derivation and composition or by some other meaning expressed the characteristics of these personages, in a word they gave them speaking names; names it was only needful to hear in order to know at once of what nature those would be who bore those names.[6]

The French comic theatre, by contrast, due in large part to the continuing powerful influence of Molière, generally remained faithful to the seventeenth-century system of conventionalized Italianate names. Thus when English, French, or German plays are translated into one of the other languages, as often occurred in the late eighteenth century, the translator must take into account this difference in onomastic codes. Destouches's comedy *Le Dissipateur* provides a good example of this. The original is peopled almost entirely by the traditional names of French comedy: Cléon, Géronte, Arisinoé, Cidalise, Floriman, Pasquin, and so on. The only possible "speaking" name is Carton, one of the hero's dissipated friends, with its suggestion of playing cards. When Gottsched translated this play into German, the names were almost entirely changed to reflect a more direct signifying code. The "wastrel" of the title, Cléon, became Herr von Lockerfeld (a *locker Gefell* being a loose-living fellow);

his false friend, originally an unnamed Le Comte, became Der Graf von Falschgrund. His other dissipated friends, Floriman and Carton, became Schmausegern (lover of banqueting) and Kartenlieb (lover of cards). The honest young widow he courts, Julie in the original, becomes literally honest (*ehrlich*) as Frau von Ehrlichsdorf, and her rival, the seductive coquette Cidalise, becomes Fräulein von Bühlwitz (spirit of love).

Neither of the English adaptations, *The Generous Imposter* and *The Spendthrift*, is as thoroughgoing as Gottsched in converting Destouches's names, but they make sufficiently striking adjustments to demonstrate the difference in English expectations on this matter. The young widow in the second remains Julia, but in the first becomes Mrs. Courtly, an adjustment close to Gottsched's. On the other hand, the first gives the hero a moderately normal name, Sir Harry Glenville, while the second calls him Moneylove. The treacherous friend in the first becomes Supple, and the other friends Holdfast and Trimbrush in the first and Florid and Piquet in the second.

One of the features of all "speaking" names, as we have noted, is that while they may indicate a general type, a profession, or an actantial role, they nevertheless always maintain a pretense of individuality. A whole series of nineteenth-century British sailors or Restoration fops with markedly similar names may be created by a single actor, who will obviously bring to them much the same interpretation, yet the varied names suggest that the audience is supposed to accept the manifestations as individual representatives of a general type. No such suggestion is present in the somewhat more abstract coding system that indicates characters simply by their profession or place in society, stressing the typical at the expense of the individual. In this sort of code a cook, instead of bearing a speaking name like Ladle or Knife, is called simply The Cook, and a doctor is called not Syringe or Scalpel but The Doctor. Strictly speaking, such characters have no names at all, since unlike the character in Albee's play, these characters are not in fact *named* Cook and Doctor, only so designated. Usually we are never told their "real" names. Instead of bearing traditional "father" and "son" names like Molière's Orgon and Damis, such characters are designated as The Father and The Son. The medieval religious drama uses this code extensively, though not exclusively, for characters added to biblical stories but not named in the Bible, such as Jailer, Messenger, Traveler, or Angel. Frequently these appear in groups of two or three, so that we find a First, Second, and Third Shepherd, or Counselor, or Torturer. In more recent times this code was revived by Strindberg, most notably in the *To Damascus* trilogy, to achieve an abstract, parablelike effect and to allow various projections of a single consciousness—The Stranger, The Beggar, The Doctor, The Pilgrim, The Tempter—to interact with one another. This coding system was passed on from Strindberg to the expressionists, whose dramas, concerned with basic family relationships and with man and technological society, often used names evoking these paradigms: The Mother, The Father, The Son, The Daughter, The Engineer, The Worker, The Boss, The Clerk.

With these non-names or generic names, indicating only a role in a social or family structure, we are near the abstract end of the drama's onomastic spectrum. A generic name like The Son, The Poet, or The Engineer still suggests an entire character, though Strindberg and others began to use such names to suggest different aspects of a single consciousness. In other periods of dramatic history an onomastic code was developed that actually split the individual into attributes, attitudes, emotions, or other abstract qualities that became personified as actants in a dramatic structure. Occasionally a body has been literally fragmented, as in Tzara's *The Gas Heart,* where Ear, Eye, Nose, and Mouth appear as characters, but generally such fragmentation takes the form of attitudes, humors, or psychological states. The medieval and Renaissance moralities and their close cousins, the interludes and chronicle plays, are the genres that offered the fullest scope to such naming systems. The virtues and vices are perhaps the most typical of such "characters"— Courage and Love, Envy and Sloth—and within the spectrum of morality names these might be considered the closest to "speaking" names. As we have already noted, it is a fairly short step from characters like Killigrew's Mr. Jolly and Mr. Sadd to morality characters like Gluttony and Wrath. In both cases a certain interpretation of the character is clearly, even baldly, suggested.

When we move to the more abstract denominations in the morality this similarity disappears. Names like Felycyte, Perseveraunce, or Cyrcumspeccyon give a distinctly less clear idea of what sort of "personality" a character bearing them might possess, and Truth, Gude Counsall, and Honest Recreation, less still. At last we come to such basic abstractions as Mankynde and Everyman, almost the polar opposites of the names of realism. From names operating at least in appearance in the same manner as those of real life, we have moved through a series of codes of increasing abstraction to these ultimate generic names in which all individuality and details of character disappear.

Beyond this it seems impossible to go, but the code system of the morality in fact allows one further abstraction, into a domain rarely encountered in the drama, the nonhuman. In the vast majority of plays the forces against which the individual struggles are represented by other individuals, but the general abstracting system of the morality allows the dramatist to bring nonhuman actants directly into the dramatic world. So Mankynd may encounter not only human friends and foes, but also Nature, Goods, or World in the form of dramatic actants. Such "characters" are clearly restricted in their actantial roles. There are no moralities that are concerned primarily with the actions or adventures of Goods or World; such figures serve always essentially as dramatic "markers," establishing positions in reference to which Mankynd is defined. Nevertheless, by moving entirely out of the realm of humanity, such names emphasize an important aspect of morality naming, which characterizes this end of the onomastic spectrum. As we move away from the names of realism, we find characters at first increasingly bound to their names and then absorbed by them. At the morality end of the spectrum characters literally are their names, and nothing more. Indeed, here even the living presence of the actor becomes a distraction through its necessary specificity. At the realistic end of the spectrum, the onomastic codes blend off into life itself, while at the morality end they blend off into the world of abstract thought, with the "names" removed entirely from humanity and becoming the signs of pure concepts.

NOTES

1. James Curtiss Austin, *The Significant Name in Terence. University of Illinois Studies in Language and Literature* VII (4).

2. Emile Zola, *Doctor Pascal,* trans. E. Z. Vizetelly (New York, 1925), x.

3. R. C. Knight, *Racine et la Grèce* (Paris, 1950), 261, 281, 319–20; Georges May, *Tragédie cornéllienne, tragédie racinienne* (Urbana, 1948), 157–64.

4. John Loftis, *The Spanish Plays of Neoclassic England* (New Haven, 1923), 54–62.

5. See Roger Herzel, *The Original Casting of Molière's Plays* (Ann Arbor, 1981).

6. Gotthold Lessing, *Hamburg Dramaturgy,* trans. Victor Lange (New York, 1962), 233.

PART TWO

The Playing Field

✳ ✳ ✳ ✳ ✳   The Semiotics of
Theatre Structures

As THE FIELD OF modern theatre semiotics has developed, many aspects of the art have been investigated from this point of view—the development of the text itself and the performance implicatives that it contains; the gestures and movements of actors; the visual and auditory signifying systems of costume, lighting, music, makeup, and so on. The major concern of such investigations, understandably, has been semiotic aspects of the text, or of the performance of the text. More recently, increasing attention has been given to the audience's contributions to this process, but the focus has naturally remained on the semiotics of the text/performance. This is quite proper, but if we really wish to consider the semiotics of an actual theatre performance, we must of course bear in mind that the performance itself, while it is the central object of investigation, is only part of the total experience of attending the theatre and of making sense of what happens when we undergo such an experience.

As early as 1943 Eric Buyssens suggested that an accurate semiotic study of an operatic performance would have to consider the communication that takes place for a few hours in an entire world, both on the stage and in the auditorium. It is hardly surprising that neither Buyssens nor any subsequent semiotician has undertaken so massive an analysis, but Buyssens' observation should serve to remind us that semiotics needs to be concerned with a considerably broader field in the analysis of theatrical performance than has normally been the case.

I would like to suggest briefly one aspect of this broader field as it might be dealt with by theatre semiotics. This is one of the richest and most significant aspects of the theatre event aside from the performance itself: the physical environment of the performance. I hope further to suggest how certain strategies already developed in the fields of architectural and urban semiotics may be of use to theatre semioticians in such analysis.

As semiotics has evolved as a field of study in Europe, one branch, pursued particularly by theorists first in Italy and subsequently in France, has considered the semiotic implications of individual architectural objects. Architectural theory in the English language has only very recently begun to turn to considerations of this sort. Late-nineteenth- and early-twentieth-century theorists placed architecture with music among the abstract, nonimitative arts, as opposed to painting, sculpture, and poetry, thus denying it any significative ability beyond its function and such abstract qualities as mass and rhythm. Max Dessoir's *Aesthetik* of 1924 spoke of poetry as an art of "definite association" and architecture as one of "indefinite associations."

Around 1960, however, a number of critics began to argue that architecture, too, has messages to convey. Sedlmayr in Germany and von Simson in England published books on the specific associations of the medieval cathedral. Hautecoeur in France offered a work on the symbolism of the circle and the cupola in architecture, and Baldwin Smith published a study with the provocative title *The Dome: A Study in the History of Ideas*. By the late 1960s books with titles like *The Language of Architecture* and *Meaning in Architecture* were appearing, preparing the way for more specifically semiotically oriented essays appearing in many journals during the next decade. An article by Marxist aesthetician Jastrebova in *Kunst und Literatur* in 1976 began boldly: "The dialectic between the changes in the organization of material structures and the organization of human society in terms of its ideas, convictions, and emotional values may be seen with particular clarity in architecture." The titles of an intriguing and controversial series of editorial-essays in the 1976–77 issues of *Architectural Review* reveal how far architectural theory had come by that time toward the acceptance not merely of architectural connotation, but also of something close to architectural communication: "What does architecture talk about?", "What does the architect say through architecture?", and "What does society say through architecture?"

Now I would like to suggest that questions of this sort should prove challenging to theatre historians as well. What do theatres talk about? What do their architects say through them? And perhaps most intriguing, what does society say through its theatres? It is important to realize that we are not speaking here exclusively, or even primarily, of the theatre's function as a place of performance. Umberto Eco clarifies this matter very well in his discussion of architecture in *La Struttura Assente* (1968). Here he suggests that a specific architectural object may be considered a sign, and like any sign is composed of a meaning (a signified), which in this case is the function fulfilled by the object (a space for dwelling, for worship, etc.) and something standing for that meaning (a signifier), which in this case is a building tied to that function by traditional cultural codes. Again like any sign, the sign thus formed is immediately open to further development by the addition of new connotations, ranging far beyond the original functional meaning. Just as a royal throne has the function of any chair—an object to sit on—but also has other and more important meanings according to its connotations, so houses and churches have primary functional meanings as dwellings and places of worship, but also a host of secondary meanings concerning the way their users relate to society as a whole, both immediately and historically. Similarly the theatre, beyond its basic function of providing a space for a public to watch a performance, will provide many additional connotative meanings to the culture of which it is a part.

Thus a semiotic perspective should urge us to consider that the theatre, an architectural object found in a wide variety of societies and historical periods, can be expected to offer a rich selection of connotations beyond its basic function of providing a space for the encounter of spectator and performance. As a way of suggesting some of the possibilities involved in viewing theatres in this way, I will consider briefly four general ways in which semiotic analysis might be profitably applied to physical theatre structures and, indeed, to performance locations in general.

Many discussions of architectural semiotics begin with a consideration of space, and this is hardly surprising. Surely no one in theatre needs to be told that space "speaks"—that spatial configurations can be powerful signifying agents. Perhaps nothing is more fundamental to architecture than the articulation of space, and indeed some architectural semioticians have argued that the semiotics of architecture should best be pursued as a part of a general semiotics of space.[1]

Few other architectural objects found in a variety of cultures have so consistent a basic spatial structure as theatre, since the very nature of theatre seems to suggest a spatial dialectic, opposing the space of the viewer to the space of the viewed. In this necessarily brief discussion I will develop a few implications of this common assumption, though before doing so I should remark that even this dialectic, generally accepted as it is, is culturally generated rather than inherent and that other arrangements are possible. Environmental theatre, for example, consciously fuses these normally opposed spaces, creating a situation which encourages audiences to experience and understand theatre in a quite different way.

In most historical periods, theatres have clustered around the two central spaces of viewer and viewed other supporting spaces for each—the "backstage" spaces which surround the actors' space and which are traditionally unseen by and off-limits to the spectators; and the various "public" spaces, such as foyers, bars, and lobbies contiguous to the auditorium, where actors traditionally are not to be seen. Violations of these spatial rules—actors in the lobbies or spectators backstage—are correspondingly highly charged symbolically. Each of these collections of support spaces serves as a kind of transitional area, a sort of vapor lock between the outside world, where actors and audience members mingle in quite different relationships, and the special world created by the juxtaposition of stage and auditorium. Both spectators and actors utilize these intermediate spaces to prepare themselves for their different "roles" in the central stage-auditorium space. Actors get into costume and makeup, and pursue whatever physical or psychological preparation they consider necessary for their entrance into the mystic space of the stage and the confrontation with the audience. The spectators make more modest but similar adjustments, checking their coats, chatting with others preparing to share the same event, reading programs, or, in the great opera houses, strolling about the lavish public spaces, removing themselves, as all these activities encourage them to do, from their concerns outside the theatre, to focus upon their impending duties and pleasures as participants in the theatrical experience. At intermissions, both actors and spectators retire to their separate and distinct worlds, where both may relax briefly with their fellows from the tension of the stage-auditorium confrontation.

A wide variety of other symbolic systems may be observed in both support areas. Backstage, for example, the relative importance of various performers is traditionally marked by the sizes and locations of their preparation areas. The "stars" may have large and well-appointed dressing areas, located near the stage, for their private use, while performers of lesser status have less space, less privacy, more stairs to climb, and so on, in close correlation with their status in the production or in the profession as a whole. Insensitivity on this matter by directors or managers has not infrequently led to serious conflicts and even to actors' withdrawing from productions. A similar, and usually much more complex, social stratification has traditionally been found in the audience support spaces, with different bars and foyers for various social ranks.

The auditorium itself is a particularly rich source of political, social, and economic signification. The possession of a box at the opera has traditionally been regarded in Western society as one of the most dependable signs of membership in the privileged classes. Indeed, the Metropolitan Opera of New York was originally built not to satisfy a passion for this art, but because the new wealth represented by the Vanderbilts, the Astors, and the Morgans was unable to obtain boxes at the old Academy of Music, where all the "aristocratic" space was already filled by the old "Knickerbocker" society: the Cuttings, Schuylers, and Van Rensselaers. Rather than settle for symbolically inferior space, the new society felt compelled to build its own theatre.[2] Although Italian opera houses from the seventeenth through the early nineteenth centuries had a variety of owners—some monarchs, some municipalities, some wealthy individuals—the seating remained hierarchical in a remarkably predictable way, easily "read" by anyone who attended these theatres. The competition for the most prestigious boxes was frequently fierce, and when the theatre was attached to a royal palace, as at Turin, the king himself might have sole authority for making these assignments. In Venice the doge had this responsibility, and the English ambassador made a formal complaint to him in 1671 about his box assignment in terms that underline the symbolism of the situation: "He did not care for music, esteem poetry, or understand the stage, but merely desired it for the honor of his office," like "his predecessor and all the other residents at present at court."[3]

The second tier of boxes (out of four, five, or six) was always the most aristocratic. The first and third enjoyed equal standing in communities where there was a large enough aristocracy to demand this. More often they were a step down, accommodating a mixture of aristocrats, lawyers, doctors, and civil servants. In 1814 the third tier of the Reggio Emilia was opened also to Jewish bankers, hitherto banned from all boxes, along with noncitizens and "mechanics." Tiers above the third were of lower status still, and when a theatre removed the partitions in the top tier to make an open gallery, this was a clear signal during the nineteenth century that a distinctly lower class of patrons was being welcomed. Such patrons were referred to at La Scala as the *minuto popolo,* but these "minor people" still included no laborers, let alone peasants; rather, they were soldiers, artisans, and providers of petty services. If persons still lower on the social scale wished to participate in the operatic experience, they had to do so, until late in the nineteenth century, by standing outside the entrances to catch what they could of the sounds from within.[4] Of course, the traditional keystone of this symbolic seating order was the royal box, placed in the center of the most favored area, directly facing the stage. Even the so-called "democratic" seating arrangement at Bayreuth did not reject a traditional royal box at the back center of the house for the sponsoring prince.

A second major area for semiotic analysis of the physical theatre often works to reinforce the messages of space. This is the area of decoration and design elements. The spatial prominence and central location of the royal box may provide its most obvious and direct architectural statement, but the canopies, crowns, cupids, and coats of arms that surround it contribute in no small way to its impact. Stendhal, giving what is essentially a brief semiotic analysis of the royal box in the Teatro San Carlo of Naples, says: "Nothing is more majestic and magnificent than the great royal box above the central door. It rests upon two golden palm-trees of natural height. The drapes are metal leaves of pale russet. Even the crown, that outdated emblem, has nothing ridiculous about it here."[5] The decorations and even the furnishings of boxes have frequently been used to communicate messages about the owner's wealth or social position. In Naples in the eighteenth century, the government became sufficently concerned with such display to enact a sumptuary law regulating the number of candles allowed in a theatre box according to the social rank of the owner. The obvious signifying potential of such a decree is revealed by a common expression of contempt in Naples at that period: "He's nothing but a one-candle gentleman."

The variety and complexity of design and decoration signification in the physical theatre are enormous. On the most direct level theatres often give specific verbal messages to their audiences—the exit signs required by safety regulations in modern theatres, the classical quotations or names of sovereigns or cultural heroes placed above the proscenium or on the fronts of boxes, the advertisements painted on the act curtains in many late-nineteenth-century American opera houses. In conjunction with these written messages are often found paintings or sculptures representing cult figures or patrons of the art. In certain historical periods, the weight of such cultural reference has become almost overwhelming. Charles Garnier boasted that he could fill a book with the allegorical figures in the new Paris Opera, suggesting that the "abundance of impressions which gush from lyric drama are complemented by the impression of abundance which gushes from the architecture." This rich elaboration was, moreover, suited in his eyes to the patrons of grand opera: "The diamonds and jewels of the one echo the marbles and gilding of the other."[6]

On another level of connotation, the selection of design elements, decorative motifs, and even colors reveals something of any theatre's desired or actual public image. The staggering prolixity of signification in Garnier's opera helped to authenticate this building as a kind of vast cultural repository, a temple to the cult of high art as it was seen by the society of late-nineteenth-century Europe. Like the medieval cathedral, it collected and displayed the whole panoply of symbolization associated with the history and performance of its now-secular ceremonies.

All sorts of social preoccupations of the time may be found in the decoration of theatres. The French national theatre, the Theatre of the Nation, was briefly closed in 1794, when its company was arrested for suspected royalist sympathies. When the theatre reopened as the Theatre of Equality, it had been purged visually of all aristocratic references. A huge democratic sweep of seats replaced the old boxes and balconies; statues of Liberty and Equality, the special aristocratic seats at the sides of the stage. Busts of Marat and other revolutionary heroes replaced those of Molière and Racine, and the gilded friezes and plaster laurel branches were painted red, white, and blue, as was the dome of the theatre. When Robespierre fell two years later, boxes and balconies were restored, and Apollo and the Muses returned to the dome. In 1808, with Napoleon the new emperor, the theatre was renamed the Theatre of the Empress, an imperial box was built in the location of the former royal one, and Napoleonic emblems surmounted the proscenium where twenty years before the royal fleur-de-lis had appeared. Thus in title, in spatial arrangements, and in decor, the national theatre reflected with scrupulous accuracy the enormous shifts in the French political scene during these turbulent years.[7]

The articulation of space and the selection and arrangement of decorative elements may thus express a wide range of information about not only a society's view of the theatre itself, but also about all manner of social, political, and economic concerns. These two areas of potential semiotic analysis of course involve only a certain, rather limited section of the public—that portion of the population which actually attends the theatre. The other two areas I would like to mention involve a far larger part of the urban population, since a theatre may also speak to an urban dweller who never attends it. We now turn from architectural semiotics to the closely related, though so far less developed, field of urban semiotics, which views the city as a "text" created by human beings in space, spoken by and speaking to those who inhabit it, move through it, and observe it, and of the roles of individual units, such as theatres, within such a text.

Certain of the concerns and approaches of this kind of study were anticipated in Kenneth Lynch's fascinating 1960 book *The Image of the City,* which considered the methods by which the inhabitants of a city mentally structure and organize their surroundings. Lynch suggested five types of elements used to "make sense" of the urban text: paths, the learned routes by which inhabitants move from one part of the city to another; edges, which act as barriers to paths and often as boundaries between two kinds of areas; districts, relatively large areas with some common characteristics; nodes, where travelers must make decisions between alternate paths; and landmarks, singular elements used for orientation.

Roland Barthes' 1965 essay "The Eiffel Tower" applies a similar strategy, in semiotic terms, to the process by which a visitor to the Eiffel

Tower makes sense of the panorama spread out beneath him. In Barthes' term, he "deciphers" this scene, applying "structuralism without knowing it." "Paris offers itself to him as an essentially *prepared* object, exposed to the intelligence, but which he must construct himself by mental activity." The viewer, Barthes continues, brings to this panorama not only an interest in physical relationships, but also in functional and connotative ones: "On the great polar axis, perpendicular to the horizontal bend of the river, three zones stacked one above another, as though along a prone body, three functions of human life; at the top, at the foot of Mont-martre, pleasure; at the center, around the Opéra, materiality, business, commerce; toward the bottom, at the foot of the Panthéon, knowledge, study; then, to the right and left, enveloping this vital axis like two pro-tective muffs, two large zones of habitation, one residential, the other blue-collar; still further, two wooded strips, Boulogne and Vincennes."[8]

Barthes' mental division of Paris into major districts, with fairly dis-tinct edges, harmonizes well with Lynch's system, even though Barthes is much more structuralist and gestaltist in orientation, emphasizing the signifying processes of opposition, alternation, and juxtaposition. Both consider how districts are encoded and distinguished by city inhabitants, each district having its own set of related connotations. Both provide stimulating suggestions for the analysis of historical and contemporary theatres in their urban context. Clearly, those theatres seeking to attract the attention and patronage of the general public will locate, whenever possible, near important nodes, along major paths, and perhaps close to prominent landmarks, while a theatre tied to a specific segment of the population will likely be found in a district congenial to that segment, either because the theatre was consciously placed there to share the connotations of the district or because, once established, it came to be associated with its district. Semiotics encourages us to consider the dif-ferent connotations of one node, one path, one district as opposed to another and to ask what urban meanings are involved in the use of any particular location.

Much attention, for example, has been given to the locations of Eliza-bethan public theatres, and all students of theatre have at least a general idea of the connotations of these locations for Elizabethan Londoners. Finsbury Fields and Bankside were politically and geographically—and, hence, socially and culturally—marginal areas, contiguous to the city but not part of it, liberties answerable only to the crown. Patrons entering these areas crossed clear boundaries—the city wall or the river—to enter a kind of ludic space, symbolically as well as physically separated from their customary world, a space both disreputable and exciting, admirably reflecting the ambiguous position held by the theatre in Elizabethan society.

Aside from the Elizabethan period, however, historians have given only the most modest attention to the urban context of historical theatres—where they were located; what other sorts of establishments, bistros, banks, or bordellos were located near them; and, ultimately, what this location and these neighbors can tell us about how the citizens of various historical periods understood the theatre as an object in the urban text. Consider, for example, Barthes' connotative map of the general zones of Paris. Theatres located within each of these zones clearly share something of the connotations of the zone as a whole. Thus the "pleasure" district of Montmarte offers variety, burlesque, and spectacular follies theatres (in the late nineteenth century, when this was more distinctly an artistic "bohemia," it was the favored locale of small experimental theatres like the Théâtre-Libre). Barthes' "materiality, business, and commerce" zone is where we today find the major boulevard houses and the Opéra. In his "knowledge, study" zone the major theatre is the Odéon, the national house devoted to new, foreign, and experimental work, and a scattering of small, intellectually sophisticated experimental ventures.

As the public respectability of theatre and of those who are involved in this art has changed, this has been faithfully reflected in the respectability of urban locations. In the early seventeenth century theatres were permitted to locate within the city of London, but their social position was still very low. The area bordering the river and the temple known as Alsatia, perhaps the shadiest district in the city, sheltered both Salisbury Court and the later Dorset Garden (with a riverfront entrance so that higher-class patrons would not have to approach it through Alsatia).

By the nineteenth century, however, theatres were no longer hidden away on dim side streets or in questionable neighborhoods, but were proudly displayed public monuments, often in the most elegant sections of the city. In his rebuilding of Paris, Baron Haussmann utilized in several locations theatres as landmark features to define the nodes of the new city. Central to his plan was the Opéra, placed in that section of Paris most associated with the upper bourgeoisie. His new boulevards linked this cultural center to specific other landmarks representing the values of his society: the cultural monuments of the Palais Royal, the Louvre, and the Arc de Triomphe, and the social monuments of the new railway stations and the stock exchange. Today's French socialist government, planning a new opera house for the lower classes to open for the bicentennial of the Revolution, has selected a site equally in tune with its own ideology: the Place de la Bastille, the center of Barthes' blue-collar residential zone, the emblem of the Revolution, the 1830 uprisings, and more recently a rallying point for Mitterrand's socialist supporters.

Other modern city planners, less consciously ideological in their concerns, have nevertheless shared this modern view of theatre as no longer a center for the gathering of undesirable elements but, on the contrary, as a device for the upgrading of the surrounding area. Clearly, this concern was reflected in the selection of the locations for London's new

National Theatre and for Lincoln Center, and recently New York has seen a much more modest new theatre row on West 42nd Street contributing to the social uplifting of this area. An interesting example of this process from almost a century ago is provided by Augustin Daly's project for a London theatre in 1891. By the mid-nineteenth century, fashionable London had moved westward from this area, leaving the district between Leicester Square and Soho a grim slum filled by immigrants and political refugees from the continent. When Daly decided to locate his theatre in this unpromising area, this was generally viewed not as a choice dictated by the low social position of the theatre, but, on the contrary, as a bold step in a long-awaited process of urban renewal. A paper of the period upbraided the government and the owners of property in the area for not cleaning up this metropolitan disgrace long since: "It is probably left to an American to do work that ought to have been done by an Englishman. When Mr. Augustin Daly takes possession of his new theatre he will clear up this muck in twenty-four hours." This prophesy proved, of course, a bit optimistic, but there is no question that the establishment of Daly's theatre in this area provided a focus for further development in the heart of what is now London's major theatre district.

The diachronic movement of theatre areas is another aspect of urban studies that should be of interest to theatre historians. Daly correctly anticipated, and perhaps encouraged, the movement of the London theatre district and its consolidation in the Leicester Square area from scattered locations to the east. Historically both London and Paris have developed slowly westward, with the more fashionable districts moving ahead of city development and leaving less desirable residential and industrial areas to the east. There is clearly a relationship between this movement and that of fashionable theatre locations. Neither eastern London nor eastern Paris has seen the establishment of such theatres, but instead more humble ethnic or working-class houses of entertainment harmonious with the connotations of their neighborhoods. This pattern has been even clearer in New York City, where the confines of Manhattan Island dictated an essentially northward expansion, and the fashionable residential areas moved gradually up the island as the city grew. The Park, the Astor Place Opera House, the Academy of Music, the Metropolitan Opera each were erected at important nodes along the Broadway path, all near open public areas and fashionable residential districts, and all marking, at the time of their construction, the northern and, thus, most aristocratic edge of the theatre and entertainment district. In the meantime, once-fashionable theatres, such as the Bowery, steadily declined in social status as the northward movement of fashionable New York left their neighborhood farther and farther behind.[9]

Finally we may turn from the signification of theatre location within the city to that of the building itself, as a unit within the urban text. The external appearance of a theatre, its shape and decorative elements, clearly provide information not only to its patrons, but also to casual passersby, about that specific organization and its offerings, and often about theatre in general within a particular society. When the opera was invented in the late Renaissance its creators proved in fact far more faithful to the cultural assumptions of their own period than to those of the classic Greek tragedy they fancied they were reviving. Nowhere is this contrast more striking than in the physical theatres created for the performance of each. Hegel, in a section of his *Aesthetics* that deals with what we might today call architectural semiotics, contrasts the architectural symbolism of the Greek temple with the romantic church. The former is "gay, open, and pleasing to the senses," a place "in direct communication with the world of external Nature," while the latter is wholly shut off from "external Nature and all the diverting occupations and interests of finite existence," a place "for an assembly of persons to concentrate their numbers in one spot shut off from the rest of the world."[10]

The contrasting architectural symbolism Hegel finds in classic and romantic religious structures is quite similar to the contrasting symbolism of classic and Renaissance theatrical structures. Greek theatres, even more strikingly than Greek temples, were open to nature and to the world, while the traditional modern theatre, from the Renaissance onward, has shut out that world as completely as possible. There are, of course, important social implications in this change. Richard Wagner in *Die Kunst und die Revolution* argued that during the late Middle Ages and the Renaissance art was appropriated as a private amusement for the rich and the powerful.[11] Architecturally, this process is confirmed by the embedding of princely theatres within royal residences, like jewels in the caskets of their owners. Nothing in fact could be more opposed to the huge open public theatres of classic times than these tiny, ornate, secluded halls, where the general public had access only by the sufferance of the prince, whose dominance of this theatre was reflected everywhere in its architecture and its decoration—in its physical location within his palace, in his coat of arms over the proscenium arch, in his lavish box dominating the center of the auditorium, and in the perspective scenery, revealing its full effect only from the vantage point of that box.

In sharp contrast to the great public monuments of classic Greece, these theatres were essentially hidden from everyone but the prince and his guests, not offering to the curious public even an identifiable external wall. A striking example of this is provided by one of the most famous of the princely theatres, that built by the Cardinal Richelieu in his palace next to the Louvre. The theatre of the Palais-Cardinal, like the building that enclosed it, was designed to reflect, in the manner already established by the court theatres in Italy, the glory of its owner. Richelieu was well aware of the symbolic uses of architecture. One of his central concerns as minister was with the continued stability of the succession, since he remembered well the sufferings France had undergone from rival claimants to the throne in the past. Thus, just as Richelieu sought to strengthen the rights of the heir apparent politically, he provided in his will for his palace, second only to the Louvre in magnificence among Parisian dwellings, to be permanently the property of the king or the crown prince, and no one else, as an architectural symbol of the succession.

When later in the century the cardinal's former theatre became the home of the national opera, it remained architecturally and politically under the control of the inhabitant of the Palais. In 1763 this theatre burned, and it was suggested that the new Opéra, as a national theatre, might be built in a more public location, preferably one separated from other buildings in case of fire. The duc d'Orléans, however, refused to give up his traditional architectural and political claim to this theatre. Moreover, he rejected several proposals that would have maintained the theatre within his palace but given it an external architectural identity. At a considerable sacrifice in convenience of internal arrangements for both theatre and palace, he insisted that the same general principle be applied to the new building as had been to the old. The theatre was incorporated into a wing built in exact parallel to another wing containing dwelling units, so that from the outside it continued to appear as nothing other than a part of his personal dwelling.[12] National opera or not, it remained visually and spatially "his" theatre.

Nonoperatic theatres of the seventeenth and early eighteenth centuries, more common in France and England than elsewhere, were as a rule almost equally modest in their external identification, tucked away into obscure urban corners. Early maps of Drury Lane and Covent Garden theatres show them crowded uncomfortably behind rows of small dwellings on almost every side, approachable only by modest passageways or minor streets. It was the continental European opera houses of the eighteenth century that established a very different idea of the theatre's possible position in the urban text. Frederick the Great's 1741 opera house in Berlin was the first major example of the new style, set in an isolated position in a great open public space, exposed and decorated on all four sides. Henceforth the idea of the opera house as a public cultural monument (despite its strong symbolic ties with the upper classes) rapidly replaced that of the opera house as the private architectural possession of the prince. The sponsors of these new opera houses, while they had little desire to admit the general urban populace into these structures, clearly desired their theatres to impress that populace and to suggest a relationship between their architectural grandeur and the cultural achievement and glory of the city, the state, and their rulers. Hence, the appearance of the state theatres as a landmark in Lynch's term, helping to define, as the Paris Opéra so clearly does, the mental map of the city. The nineteenth-century state opera house or theatre in its monumentality and architectural isolation thus had important ties to such monuments as the great public museums of that era or the triumphal arches of the classic period.

The position in the urban text taken by such structures contrasts sharply with that being established at approximately the same time by the more entrepreneurial commercial theatres. Architecturally and spatially these joined the world of commerce, appearing in their most typical form as simply one more structure in the facade row of the modern urban streetscape. The French term "théâtre du boulevard" clearly reflects this type of urban articulation. Only one wall of the theatre is displayed for the inhabitants of the city, an ornamental facade that takes its place among a series of other contiguous facades composing one side of a modern street or boulevard. This architectural arrangement was developed in early modern times primarily to serve the needs of commercial shops. The potential customer moves along a commercial street as she moved along the rows of booths and stalls in the medieval market or in the present-day Middle Eastern souks, past a series of goods displayed for sale.

The theatre has joined this commercial world only at the price of considerable architectural contortion. The importance of having an attractive facade on the commercial street makes that frontage very expensive and thus encourages a series of long, narrow buildings, a suitable arrangement for shops but not at all for theatres, especially theatres seeking a large public that will pay more for seats convenient to the stage. The result has usually been a facade with no true relationship to the actual shape or structure of the commercial theatre, which probably lies hidden behind neighboring buildings. Even the fenestration, when it exists, is largely decorative, providing little information about the actual use of the building. All of this, however, makes the street facade potentially a very interesting subject for semiotic analysis, since its major function is information-bearing, to present a particular public image to the passing citizenry.

Exterior decoration of theatres, like interior decoration, has often favored the period's idea of high fashion—neoclassicism at the beginning of the nineteenth century, the Mansard style and neobaroque toward the end, the clean sweeping lines of modernism and art deco in the early years of our own century. Classic Greek columns, pediments, and pilasters have always been popular, not because of associations with the Greek theatre, which in fact used few such elements, but because they suggest classic achievement and aesthetic respectability. Architectural codes, iconographic and spatial, provide the best general tools for the analysis of theatre facades, but they by no means exhaust the vocabulary of such exteriors. The inscription "For the People" over the doors of the remodeled Theatre of Equality in 1793 and the statue of the goddess of equality between these doors attempted to send the same messages to passing citizens as did the democratic seating arrangements and tricolor banners within. The various ways in which the particular production being offered within may be announced on the facade also provide a rich area for analysis.

The vocabulary of theatre facades changes not only historically, but also geographically. An English visitor to New York in 1867 found it difficult to identify the theatres, so different was their appearance from their European counterparts: "With some few exceptions the American theatres are not distinguishable from the surrounding houses until a close proximity reveals the name, lights, and other outside paraphernalia of a place of amusement; for on either side the spacious entrance are usually to be found shops or cafes and above the windows of a hotel or retail store."[13]

Several questions are suggested by observations of this sort. What are the identifying devices of theatres in different nations and historical periods, and what does the selection of these rather than others tell us about these theatres? How do citizens of a city know that a given structure is a theatre, and not a bank or hotel? To what extent do theatres share an architectural vocabulary that relates them to other buildings, public or private, and what does this suggested relationship reveal of the theatre's aims or pretensions?

In recent years the concerns of theatre history have steadily broadened, to begin to take account of the entire social, cultural, and economic system of which theatre is a part. Already the gain in our understanding of the play, the performer, and the enacted event has been much enriched by this broader perspective. When we speak of theatre buildings, however, we still tend to speak of them in the traditional terms of theatre research, tracing such matters as the rise of the Italianate stage, the ups and downs in the fortunes of the forestage, the development of the illusionistic stage of the nineteenth century, limiting ourselves, even in these areas, to chronicling the changing and somewhat whimsical fashions of the theatre as a largely isolated social phenomenon. Other questions concerning the theatre as a constructed object in different periods and locations have scarcely been explored at all—how theatres relate architecturally to other buildings of the same period, why they utilize the particular vocabulary of ornamentation they do, where they are located in the city and what this location implies, how they relate to other parts of the urban text, or how the same theatre, in different historical periods, will take on different associations as the urban area around it changes. The pursuit of questions such as these, for most of which architectural and urban semiotics can provide us with at least preliminary research models, should provide important new insights into the theatre, not as an isolated cultural phenomenon but as a part of the rich fabric of human society.

NOTES

1. See, for example, Maria Scalvani, *L'architettura come semiotica connatativa* (Milan, 1975).

2. Eaton Quaintaine, *The Miracle of the Met* (New York, 1968), 2–3.

3. Jon Rosselli, *The Opera Industry in Italy from Cimarosa to Verdi* (Cambridge, 1984), 41.

4. *Ibid.*, 42–46.

5. Stendhal, *Rome, Naples, et Florence*, vol. 4 of *Oeuvres complètes* (Paris, 1951), 212.

6. Charles Garnier, *Le nouvel Opéra*, 2 v. (Paris, 1881), 1:24.

7. Marvin Carlson, *The Theatre of the French Revolution* (Ithaca, 1966), 199–200.

8. Roland Barthes and André Martin, *La tour Eiffel* (Paris, 1965), 43.

9. See Mary Henderson, *The City and the Theatre* (New York, 1973).

10. G. W. F. Hegel, *The Philosophy of Fine Art*, trans. F. P. B. Osmaston, 3 vol. (London, 1920), 3:80–92.

11. Richard Wagner, *Gesammelte Schriften und Dichtungen* (Leipzig, 1871–72), 3:19.

12. Victor Champier, *Le Palais-Royal d'après les documents inédits*, 2 vol. (Paris, 1900), 1:374–78.

13. Quoted in Henderson, *The City*, 121.

✳ ✳ ✳ ✳ ✳   The Old Vic:
                 A Semiotic Analysis

THE TRADITIONAL AREAS of dramatic analysis—the written text and then the theatrical performance of that text and its reception by an audience—have so far constituted almost the entire body of semiotic analysis of theatre, and not inappropriately, since it is obviously these elements which make up the core of the theatre experience. Nevertheless, semiotics has the potential to contribute a broader and richer analysis of this subject than it has yet done by heeding the concerns of those theorists more influenced by anthropological and sociological concerns, who have observed that the text-performance-audience interaction should not be studied in a vacuum, but as an event embedded in a complex matrix of social and cultural codes, all of which "communicate" or help to give a performance its particular "meaning" to its participants.

So long as we consider theatre only as the presentation of a text (or even a nontextual creation) on a stage, we remain confined to the codes and cultural expectations of that stage area. As soon as we begin looking at the theatre event as a whole, however, our analysis must expand to include many generally neglected elements of the event. Perhaps the most obvious of these are the ways in which the physical surroundings of the performance—usually a theatre building—frame and condition interpretation, and more generally the effects of the physical location of this building within the city and the pattern of theatregoing associated with this theatre.

As a way of illustrating some of the possibilities opened by analyses of this sort, I would like to focus upon a single famous theatre structure—the Old Vic of London—considering some of the ways in which this theatre, whatever plays it may have been presenting, communicated various messages to its actual and potential publics, and how these in turn contributed to establishing the contextual world in which the performances themselves were seen and understood. We shall consider such matters as interior spatial arrangements, decoration, attempts at projecting particular public images, and situation within the urban text of London, both synchronically (considering how the theatre related to its neighborhood at specific periods) and diachronically (considering how the public "interpretation" of the Vic altered as its surroundings changed).

We may begin our analysis with that feature of a theatre most familiar to the general public: its name. In 1818, when the present Old Vic opened, there was already a clearly established onomastic code for London theatres. In theory, only two theatres in London were legitimate, those whose owners held the patents granted 150 years before by Charles II. By 1818, four theatres claimed this privilege: Drury Lane, Covent Garden, Haymarket, and the English Opera, each of which prefaced its name with "Theatre Royal." Two rival houses with no such claim—the King's Theatre and the Royal Circus—still attempted an onomastic relationship with the rest. Two smaller houses, the Sans Pareil and the Sans Souci, attempted instead to give an impression of continental sophistication. Only remote Sadler's Wells took its name simply from its location.

The new theatre gained permission through one of its organizers, John Thomas Serres, who was marine painter to the king, to take a name as impressive as any in London, the Royal Coburg, even though it had no official subsidy or privilege. Its district was still so undeveloped and remote from London consciousness that such possible names as the Royal Waterloo or the Royal Lambeth would have been more comic than impressive, but Coburg was an onomastic coup, making it the only London theatre with an actual royal name. Princess Charlotte of Wales, the only daughter of the prince regent, married Prince Leopold of Saxe-Coburg just months before the first stone of the new theatre was laid.

In fact, the name "Coburg" before long became irrelevant if not embarrassing. Princess Charlotte died in childbirth before the theatre opened, Prince Leopold became king of the Belgians and disappeared from the British scene, the aging and ill William IV became king, and the nation's interest shifted to young Princess Victoria. Under these changed circumstances, the new lessees of the theatre in 1833 successfully negotiated for a new sign of court interest and proudly announced that the theatre would be rechristened the Royal Victoria, a name soon popularly shortened to the "Vic." In 1871 the first complete remodeling of the building was commemorated by a change of name to the Royal Victoria Palace Theatre, a name denounced as foolishly pompous in *The Builder,* a contemporary architectural journal.[1]

The new theatre did not succeed and stood vacant at the end of the decade, when it was taken over by representatives of the temperance movement seeking to establish an alcohol-free place of entertainment for the working classes. Thus the theatre became the Royal Victoria Coffee and Music Hall, its title declaring its allegiance to the new movement. As emphasis shifted from temperance concerns to public lectures and education at the building, "Coffee" disappeared from the title and it became in the early twentieth century the Royal Victoria Hall. For a time just before the First World War, under the influence of the Volksbühne movement in Germany, the playbills of the theatre bore the title "The People's Opera, Play, and Lecture House," but Lillian Baylis, who took over the venture in 1912, wished to emphasize conventional dramatic entertainment again, and in 1916 she wrote to the City Parochial Foundation, "We are asked on all sides to call the Vic its old title of Theatre, as Hall is harmful to the work."[2] This same year the name "Old Vic," long a popular local name for the theatre, began to appear on the programs for Shakespearian revivals, and in 1918, the centenary year, it became (and remains) the theatre's official title. Even during the years between 1963 and 1976, when the Vic was the temporary home of the embryonic National Theatre, its official title was still the National Theatre at the Old Vic.

When one turns from the name of a theatre to the architectural object, the semiotics of this object can be considered in a number of ways. The most obvious of these are the implications of location (what the physical surroundings and the position in the urban text mean to the theatre's public), implications of the articulation of space within the building itself, and the variety of messages it communicates to the public through its interior and exterior decoration. Of these, location is perhaps the most important. The theatre is an urban structure, and its particular place in the urban text at a particular time or in a particular city invariably reveals much of that theatre's public image. The major modern cities with a strong theatrical life invariably possess a theatre "district" with certain distinctive features, and that district in turn imposes a certain image upon the theatres located within it. The theatres of London's "West End" have many features in common with one another and with those of similarly located "Boulevard" theatres in Paris and "Broadway" theatres in New York (a district name applied to theatres almost none of which are, in fact, located on that street). A certain type of theatrical offering has become so identified with such theatres that their geographical location has in turn become a generic title, so that one may speak of Broadway musicals, or Boulevard or West End comedies.

Theatres outside the commercial and entertainment hub of major cities cannot hope to compete with theatres of this type by offering similar fare, and those that have succeeded in modern times have generally done so by creating one of two other sorts of public image: either that of the frankly local neighborhood theatre, catering to the needs and interests of its proximate public, or that of the specialized experimental theatre, offering unique fare attractive enough to inspire an interested public to take the extra trouble to seek it out. Both of these strategies have been employed by various directors of the somewhat remote Old Vic during the more than a century and a half of its existence.

The site of the Old Vic was determined largely by considerations of public access, as is usually the case with public structures like theatres even outside the center of a city. In Shakespeare's day, the South Bank of the Thames was the district most associated with leisure activity, despite the formidable barrier offered by the Thames, access being provided from the city only by London Bridge and by boat. This marginality of physical location reflected the marginality of theatre itself in the social system, sharing its location with other such suspect activities as bearbaiting arenas and the famous London stews. With their improved social position after the Restoration, theatres moved into more respectable London locations, particularly into what is still the city's theatre hub, the West End.

Only a limited number of theatres were officially allowed within the city, however, and the building of Blackfriars Bridge in the 1760s encouraged some theatre entrepreneurs to look again south of the river. An important node was created where the road from Blackfriars Bridge crossed that to Westminster Bridge, marked by a landmark, the Obelisk. A small commercial district sprang up here, at its center the Surrey Theatre, built in 1782. The site was a good one in terms of intersecting major paths, but it was far from major settled areas and from the main entertainment district. The opening of Waterloo Bridge in 1817 markedly changed the configuration of this area. The new bridge led directly from the heart of the entertainment district across the river, and a new road, Waterloo, led directly from it to the Surrey node. The improved access led to a rental increase at the Surrey in one year from 200 guineas to 4,200 pounds!

Halfway between the bridge and the Surrey node, however, the laying out of The Cut created another, even more attractive node, where the Royal Coburg was now erected. It was a location rich in promise, but still underdeveloped and a bit speculative. A common jest of the 1820s was that the only places Waterloo Bridge led to were Bedlam Hospital and the Royal Coburg theatre. The Lambeth Marshes not only discouraged building in this area, but also had a bad reputation as criminal haunts, and early playbills for the theatre contain the significant note, "Extra patrols are engaged for the Bridge and Roads leading to the theatre and particular attention will be given to Lighting the same."[3]

Such measures seem to have reassured patrons, for the Coburg during the next decade attracted a varied public from across the river, including fashionable aristocracy and occasionally even royalty. The area around The Cut began to be drained and developed, providing homes for workers and, indeed, for many theatre persons. George Davidge, lessee of the Coburg in 1826, had a house in nearby Charlotte Terrace, and St. George's Circus sheltered so many artists that it was known as the "theatrical barracks."[4] The theatre's neighbors were now small shops and moderately comfortable houses with front gardens, but the development of the area did little to improve its social image, and the fashionable society that came in the early years soon abandoned the house to its working-class neighbors. Later in the century the historian Edward Walford suggested that this change was not only inevitable, but also had in fact been foreseen by the builders of the theatre. In his opinion, the Coburg was erected "with a due regard to the character of the population by which it was surrounded, and was therefore designed for melodramas and pantomimes."[5]

In fact, Davidge at least made a devoted, if ultimately futile, effort to gain the Coburg a niche in the world of bourgeois entertainment, observing in a pamphlet of 1831 that "the supporters of the theatre are not those they used to be—the late hours introduced into fashionable life prevent the aristocracy being the patrons of the drama: that honor has merged into the more intelligent though perhaps less affluent class, England's staple children, wrongly termed the middle class."[6] For such a public, most members of which did not possess their own coaches, the theatre's location was a problem, but Davidge attempted to ameliorate this by establishing box offices in such bourgeois haunts as the Royal Exchange, Whitefriars, Westminster, Covent Garden, and Kensington Lane.

The gradually declining reputation of the Lambeth area undermined all such efforts and presented a formidable challenge to Davidge's successors, Abbot and Egerton (who renamed the theatre the Royal Victoria). Conditions on the stage and in the house were improved, as was transportation. Special sixpenny Red Rover omnibuses came over Waterloo Bridge every evening just before curtain and again at half-price time. Respectable society and even, on one notable occasion, Princess Victoria herself attended the theatre, but the social and urban dynamics ensured that the Royal Victoria could not continue to attract such a public. The young Charles Dickens reported on the district around the Victoria in the early 1830s, on streets presenting an appearance of dirt and discomfort "which the groups who lounge about in them in no degree tend to diminish." The ragged urchins who inhabit these streets are revealed as enthusiastic patrons of the Victoria, amusing themselves with "theatrical converse, arising out of their last half-price visit to the Victoria gallery."[7] The genteel spectators from across the river soon abandoned the Victoria to such local supporters, and in 1840 F. G. Tomlin's *Brief View of the London Stage* observed of the theatre: "situated in one of the worst neighborhoods, its audience are of the lowest kind."[8]

The opening of Waterloo Station in 1846 encouraged the further commercialization of this area and the proliferation of slum dwellings, a common fate of the areas around nineteenth-century railway terminals, all of which reinforced the association in the public mind between the Victoria and the corruption of its physical surroundings. The operation of urban semiotics can be clearly seen in such associations, whether authors felt that the corruption spread outward from the theatre (like Charles Knight, who claimed in the *Penny Magazine* of 1846 that theatres like the Victoria "have given a taint to the very districts they belong to")[9] or spread to the theatre from outside (like Charles Kingsley, who spoke of the Victoria as "a licensed pit of darkness, a trap of temptation, profligacy and sin" attended by the "beggary and rascality" of "the neighboring gin-palaces and thieves' cellars.")[10]

During the next twenty years the area around the theatre grew more commercial, but scarcely more attractive to genteel playgoers. The dwellings along The Cut disappeared, to be replaced by street stalls offering fresh fish and vegetables; old clothing stores; hairdressing salons; and steaming cookshops offering sheep's heads, pig's ears, chitterlings, and currant pudding. A few doors down from the Victoria on the same side of the road was a huge tailoring emporium, Grove's, which provided clothing to the actors in exchange for free advertising.[11] The development of The Cut and of Waterloo Road as commercial district brought many potential patrons into the Victoria's area, but it also brought competition better suited to the desires and the financial means of these patrons. Vacant shops began to be cheaply converted into inexpensive melodrama houses, the notorious Victorian "penny gaffs," which sprang up all along The Cut and Lower Marsh Road. Further competition was offered by an only slightly better class of establishments, which mixed "gaffish" melodramas with music-hall turns. The corner of York and Waterloo Road became a standard gathering place for actors seeking temporary employment among these unstable operations, the general success of their endeavors being suggested by the popular names then applied to the area, "Poverty Corner" and "Misery Junction." Unable to attract audiences to its rather more respectable entertainments, and equally unable, due to its size and expenses, to compete with the "gaffs" on their own territory, the Victoria was driven several times into bank-ruptcy before it was taken over in 1880 by the temperance reformers. Those very associations which so appalled the bourgeois authors of the period were precisely what made the Victoria the first choice of the reformers for a temperance music hall. Here in the center of urban vice, poverty, and degradation was where their efforts could be best employed. Middle- and upper-class patrons were no longer sought. Some came, but normally out of interest in the hall's new uplifting work, as a modern churchgoer might visit a missionary station in Africa.

In fact, the Victoria's neighborhood steadily improved toward the end of the century. The New Cut became a major market and commercial street possessing more than two hundred shops, with perhaps another one hundred twenty vendors' stalls appearing during market hours.[12] In the early twentieth century this was the ninth-busiest of more than one hundred London street markets, its noise and bustle becoming a real problem to performers in the theatre. The Victoria was still remote from central London, but its district was now more favorably regarded and lively, even a bit exotic. When the naphtha lamps were lighted over the vivid splashes of color of the fruit and vegetables in the stalls, reports Winifred Isaac, it was "one of the most romantic spots in London. Men from all parts of the world, back in town again, rubbed elbows with the costers, and, with the wind in a certain quarter and a certain amount of imagination, you could faintly smell the sea."[13] Public access steadily improved also, with the opening of the Waterloo and City underground in 1898 and the Bakerloo line in 1907, connecting Waterloo station with other parts of the city, including the theatrical West End.

Successful theatres outside major theatre districts have, as we have noted, generally achieved success either by appealing to local tastes or by offering special attractions unavailable in the city center. The Vic, having long followed the first course, turned around in 1914 to the second, becoming London's leading home of Shakespeare and opera, and as such continued to attract a public into this still-marginal area. At the same time, other urban forces were working on a larger scale to change the associations of this entire area. As early as 1907 William Archer and Harley Granville-Barker in a prophetic book, *A National Theatre: Schemes and Estimates,* suggested the South Bank as the appro-priate site for such a venture, and at last, during the Second World War, there began to be talk in goverment circles of a great public development in this area, with a national theatre as its core. After the war, the South Bank development assumed a central role in London planning, called by one history "London's Brasilia, a conscious attempt to alter London's pattern of social life by altering its geography."[14] The location of the Old Vic, as well as its reputation as a people's theatre and a theatre associated with Shakespeare, made it an inevitable component of these plans. Only a few of the strongest devotees of the old theatre thought

that as a physical structure it had the size or splendor to itself become the national theatre; but, suitably refurbished, it served for thirteen years as the temporary home of the new company while the development was being built, and for a time it seemed that the Old Vic itself would serve as the proscenium theatre for the new arts complex. When this plan did not materialize, the South Bank complex turned its back, both literally and figuratively, on the Old Vic. The large and sprawling complex has fulfilled its planners' dreams of making this area a cultural center for the city, but the center is oriented toward the river, with sweeping glass facades and esplanades, while the urban area behind it, which includes the Old Vic, remains little-developed. Paradoxically, the Old Vic, though only a few blocks from the new development, is not related to it in terms of urban semiotics and thus still seems isolated and remote. The plentiful signs in the South Bank complex, guiding visitors to its many parts and to nearby transportation, omit any reference to the nearby Old Vic, and indeed no convenient path connects it to the complex. Its future success, therefore, apparently will depend as before on establishing a unique image that will attract patrons not only from the West End, but also from the perceptually almost equally remote South Bank.

When we turn from denomination and location to specific features of the building itself, to architectural communication, our major concerns are with the articulation of space and the choice of decorative detail. According to Bentley's minimal definition, theatre occurs when one who performs pretends to be another while a third watches.[15] A certain basic spatial configuration is here already implied—a space for the active "pretender" facing a space for the passive "watcher." Thus the traditional theatre building may be seen as an enclosure for these opposed spaces (the stage and the auditorium) at its heart, with a variety of secondary support spaces (such as dressing rooms and lobbies) serving as bridges between these and the outside world. The spectator areas of Western theatres have always clearly reflected certain political, social, and economic configurations of their societies; and the Coburg, designed at the opening of the nineteenth century, followed in this respect the prevailing codes of the previous era. A fairly wide spectrum of British society attended the theatre during the eighteenth century, but exactly where they sat there was as clear a sign of their social rank as the clothing they wore or the transportation they utilized to arrive there. The highest social ranks, as on the continent, sat in the boxes (usually with a further internal ranking there). In the pit were members of the middle classes, while the galleries above the boxes were the domain of footmen, grooms, and all the less-respectable members of society. Nor was this differentiation restricted to the seating. Each of these areas had its own entrance from the street, and once inside, audience members shared no common space except the auditorium itself. Box patrons would normally enter by a center door in the front of the building (usually provided, as at the

Coburg, with a portico to shelter them as they left their coaches) into a foyer provided with a cloakroom, then ascend a staircase to one or more upper foyers or salons where they could relax at intermissions and from which extended the corridors leading to their boxes. Pit patrons entered a corridor leading directly to that area, and often, as at the Coburg, had a more modest salon of their own at the rear of the pit. Gallery patrons entered by a third door and ascended a winding staircase to their upper regions, and at intermissions generally had no option but to remain where they were or to descend again to the street. The first facade of the Coburg placed all three of these entrances in the front, but the first remodeling moved the inferior gallery entrance around to the side of the building into Webber Street.

As the social role of this theatre changed along with the codes of theatrical space in general, this traditional eighteenth-century configuration naturally changed as well. The box, pit, gallery division of seating remained essentially intact even when the theatre became, in Victorian times, essentially a one-class house, partly due to the power of this traditional arrangement and partly because a series of managers still hoped to bring back upper-class patrons to fill the empty boxes. In the meantime, alterations of the interior greatly increased the proportional size of the gallery, the domain of the theatre's most dedicated patrons.

The basic interior decoration of the original Coburg used colors and elements standard for theatres of the time and considered to represent quiet classical elegance—white bas-reliefs of masks, lyres, and military gear on fawn-color backgrounds, connected by garlands of gilded foliage, fronted the lower boxes, while the gallery offered a chaste imitation of a Grecian sculpted frieze. For decorations more obvious to the public eye, however, Serres sought emblems more specifically evocative of his own interests and of the theatre's royal connections. Portraits of the prince of Saxe-Coburg and Princess Charlotte were displayed in the main foyer of the theatre, and the act curtain showed Claremont House, their residence. After the death of Princess Charlotte her portrait in the foyer was augmented by traditional horticultural emblems of grief: cypresses and weeping willows. But within a few years this portrait had been removed and the prince remained alone, just as his name appeared alone as patron on the early playbills. Serres' own background was reflected in the most-advertised interior feature, a "grand panoramic Marine Saloon" of his creation. On one side of this was a marine allegory showing Neptune in a lavish chariot drawn by a seahorse, guided by tritons (one of whom carried an admiralty flag), and attended by boys on dolphins. The discreet display of naval chauvinism offered by this panel was made much more explicit by a balancing scene showing a recent marine triumph, the bombardment of the pirate stronghold of Algiers by Lord Exmouth in 1816. Finally Serres attempted to blend his marine interests with the actual function of the building in a painting of Shakespeare's cliff at Dover behind a harbor scene, the first of many semiotic references to Shakespeare in the history of this theatre's decoration.

Serres also designed a facade for the new theatre, a chinoiserie fantasy with dragons, pagoda roofs, and bells, a creation much more reflective of the Oriental whimsicality of the Regency Court than of contemporary architectural taste in general. Like Drury Lane, a theatre with much closer ties to the court, the original Coburg temporarily featured little Chinese canopies over the first tier of boxes, but Serres' elaborate facade proved too expensive, and a plain facade with modest neoclassic trim was created by architect Rudolph Cabanal, who designed the framework of the building. There was no portico at first, simply a row of doors on street level giving separate entrances to box, pit, and gallery seating (as a sign over each appropriate door informed the public). Above these doors a legend running the width of the facade certified the legitimacy of the establishment: "Licensed pursuant to act of Parliament of the twenty-fifth of King George the Third." Next came a row of tall, thin windows, then the raised letters of the title "Royal Coburg Theatre," then a smaller row of windows with rounded tops, and finally a simple broken pediment to give the whole a modest classic touch. The side along Waterloo Road was of equal simplicity—three levels with a suggestion of arches in the brickwork above each window. Subsequent redesignings of the theatre continued to treat it as a conventional-facade house, de-spite this long, exposed Waterloo side, so that despite the several changes in the Cut facade, the sides of the theatre are still essentially as Cabanal designed them.

Architectural and design elements were considered at least in the early years of the Coburg as attractions potentially as great as any per-formance offered. The first bill of the theatre gave much more promi-nence to the "Superb Central Lustre" and the Marine Saloon than to the evening's plays, and the management subsequently offered in the Saloon a "PHUSEOZELOMATA, exhibiting a highly finished view of Venice with upwards of 500 figures,"[16] and probably the theatre's most famous feature, a "Looking Glass Curtain," filling the proscenium arch and weighing some five tons. This curtain, though used only a few times and then taken down because of its strain on the building's framework, be-came, as we shall see, an important element in the visual tradition of this theatre. In 1822 another marine painter, Clarkson Stanfield (later the scene painter at Drury Lane), provided new panoramic views for the main foyer, to which Cabanal added casts from statues by Canova in classic alcoves and a bust of Shakespeare, the only one of these early decorations to remain in the theatre today.

In 1824 a new manager, Watkins Burroughs, so extensively re-decorated the auditorium as to make it what he advertised (in an attempt at continental sophistication): a "Nouvelle Feature." These advertise-ments stressed the twin virtues of taste and splendor, claiming that the new decorations "unite the utmost magnificence with the most chaste and classical purity of design." In fact the box decorations, though refurbished, were little changed, the major visual adjustment being a newly designed proscenium, above which was now to be seen "Brittania, supported by Thalia and Melpomene evoking the aid of Apollo on this establishment."[17] The muses of comedy and tragedy, traditional figures, were easily read by the public, but Britannia seems to have been more ambiguous. An 1826 account of the theatres of London cautiously identifies her as "an allegorical figure (probably the Melo-dramatic Muse) holding a tablet, on which the exterior of the theatre is depicted."[18] Some engravings of the theatre in the 1830s show a similarly ambiguous (and nowhere identified) female figure in the center of Cabanal's broken pediment on the facade. An additional, and much more specific, national emblem was added to the facade sometime in the last years of the theatre's career as the Royal Coburg. A portico with Tuscan columns was erected before the facade, the front of it bearing the legend concerning the license, and above its center, the royal coat of arms with the lion and unicorn provided a readily recognized sign of the building's claim to "royal" status.

The portrait of Saxe-Coburg had long since disappeared from the lobby when, in 1833, the theatre became the Royal Victoria. No portrait of Victoria marked this transition, but the interior decoration was again touched up, and the proscenium, traditionally the major bearer of appropriate emblematic devices, marked the theatre's return to royal patronage by replacing Britannia with a royal crown on a crimson cushion. Behind it were four flags: the royal standard, the Union Jack, the American Stars and Stripes, and a fourth identified in no extant sources. "Royal Victoria," of course, also replaced "Royal Coburg" on Cabanal's otherwise unchanged facade. Soon after this refurbishment a reinstallation of the famous Looking Glass Curtain was attempted and again abandoned. This time, however, the pieces were saved and placed as decorative elements in the interior of the boxes, where they served as elegant visual reminders of this spectacular feature.

The declining fortunes of the theatre during the mid-nineteenth century were faithfully, if unconsciously, reflected in its fixtures. No longer did hopeful new managers regularly refurbish the interior. Instead the decorations of 1833 gradually fell into a desuetude which sent its own message to visitors to the house. John Hollinshead in *Ragged Life in London* found the Victoria a suitable cadre for its shabby clientele: "the fittings faded, the walls smeared with greasy dirt, the pit floor muddied and half covered with broken bottles."[19]

Matters finally came to such a pass by 1870 that major renovation was necessary simply to keep the building habitable. In 1871 the architect Jethro Thomas Robinson began the most extensive remodeling the theatre had yet seen, involving the entire interior and the facade. At last the now quite anachronistic eighteenth-century seating arrangements were altered to reflect the present social orientation of the theatre. A sweeping gallery, the new "dress circle," replaced the old aristocratic first tier, and a second large gallery replaced the old second tier and gallery above it. Dress-circle patrons still had exclusive use of the central foyer on the ground floor and an elegant double staircase to the former Marine Saloon above, but the pit was now provided with its own promenade. Sections of the old Looking Glass Curtain still embellished the walls of the pit, dress circle, and saloon.

The new facade, much more elegant than Cabanal's, employed the architectural codes of Victorian neoclassicism to give the building a solid and highly respectable public front. Huge pilasters at the sides supported a classic frieze and entablature, at the center of which appeared the name of the theatre. Atop this entablature were four large ornamental urns and, at the center, the queen's coat of arms in silhouette against the sky. Cabanal's fenestration remained, but with classic trim; his upper arched windows now flattened to support shouldered Greek architraves; and his tall, unadorned, rectangular lower windows converted into a series of Palladian archways (incidentally bringing them into better visual harmony with the brick arches and pilasters of the unchanged Waterloo side).

When the Victoria was converted into a temperance music hall little was done to improve the auditorium, since the new management wished to attract precisely that somewhat disreputable public which frequented the old and rather rough melodrama house. Most of the seating thus remained crude and inexpensive—wooden benches covered with oil-cloth for easy cleaning. The most elegant feature of the building was also its symbolic center, the coffee tavern, located at the front of the ground floor in the space of the old foyer. At one end of this was a handsome refreshment bar, fitted up by one of the venture's patrons in memory of her recently deceased son.[20] The other major ornament of the tavern was a statue of Queen Victoria. Above the tavern, the former Marine Saloon was converted into a temperance lecture hall, and these two major aristocratic spaces of the theatre were made democratic, even public, since they were open to all at hours when the theatre itself was closed. The loss of such spaces, and the opening of the pit and even the boxes by a general leveling and lowering of prices, gradually removed the original social messages of the theatre's auditorium, to bring it more to resemble the "People's Theatre" that the Vic came to be called in the early twentieth century. As the functions of the building changed from theatrical to educative, the conversion of the saloon into a lecture hall was followed by more radical conversions backstage, as dressing and scenery areas became libraries and classrooms. The growth of Morley College, named for its principal benefactor, Samuel Morley, was threatening to crowd the theatre out entirely when, in 1922, Sir George Dance provided the funds for the college to relocate and the Vic to focus again on drama.

In the meantime the public image of the Vic had undergone major changes. Both the temperance movement and the public interest in music-hall entertainment waned in the early years of the new century. The coffee tavern was replaced by a professional restaurant managed by John Pearce and Emma Cons' successor, Lilian Baylis, and the Victoria Hall Foundation began to seek new offerings more oriented toward the program of social and cultural uplift now associated with the Vic. Opera sung in English and the plays of Shakespeare now became the bases of the repertoire. This cultural cachet and a stability unmatched by any other London theatre during the war years began to attract some of London's best actors as well as a new bourgeois public to the theatre. The Vic's emphasis on Shakespeare and its refusal to cancel performances even during air raids gave it an association with patriotic pride that further enhanced its new image. The story was widely circulated of how the audience rose to a standing ovation when, on the opening night of *King John,* during a raid, Falconbridge gave the line, "This England never did, nor never shall / Lie at the proud foot of a conquerer." This quotation was subsequently placed over the proscenium arch, where it remained until the end of the war.[21]

In 1918, the unique patriotic associations of the Vic were signified by the selection of this theatre as the location for a roll of honor listing war dead from the London theatre world. The roll, placed over the Vic's stage door, was made of timber from the ship *Britannia,* and a contest was held for the most appropriate quotation from Shakespeare to complete the memorial. That selected was from *Cymbeline:* "The benediction of these covering heavens / Fall on their heads like dew; for they are worthy / To inlay heaven with stars."

The new aura of patriotism and cultural respectability attracted to the theatre in the postwar years a faithful, cohesive, and largely bourgeois audience. The public areas were gradually upgraded to suit this new public, although the main foyer could not be reworked until John Pearce's lease ran out in 1927. During the 1920s, however, floors were carpeted, tip-up seats were installed in the dress circle, and the last vestiges of aristocratic seating, the remaining boxes, were removed to enlarge the gallery and circle and to provide fire exits. Perhaps most significant, in terms of architectural semiotics, the theatre now possessed a bar—before the war it had been the only London theatre lacking that feature. Perhaps nothing else marked so clearly the change from the temperance hall of Emma Cons to the theatre of modern times.

The enshrining of Shakespeare as the patron saint of the theatre also had its effect on interior decor. His bust was placed in the main saloon, where it was decorated at an annual birthday celebration with bay and rosemary and with gold and black ribbons. The stage also was rebuilt in the early 1920s to suggest something closer to an Elizabethan performance space. Footlights were removed and a platform built out over the orchestra, framed by a false proscenium in black velvet containing traditional proscenium doors. This Elizabethan ambiance, at least in the performing areas, was further developed in the 1930s by Tyrone Guthrie, who demolished the previous proscenium and introduced a permanent set according to Shakespearian production ideas of the time, with a balcony upstage center, approached by stairs on either side and with a curtained recess beneath.

The removal of John Pearce's restaurant from the front of the Vic allowed a complete redesigning of the facade in 1927. Above the facade, the relief of the royal coat of arms was retained, but beneath that only the fenestration remained of the previous facade, the upper row becoming now a series of simple squares and ornate molded pediments placed over the tall lower windows instead of the Palladian arches. The projecting area which had contained the restaurant now enclosed a handsome foyer decorated in the rather geometric style favored between the wars. At the rear of the foyer a large engraving depicted The Cut and also the theatre as it had appeared before this latest redecoration. Outside, above the entrances to this new foyer, large incised letters designated the theatre at last as "THE OLD VIC," a name repeated on a projecting sign at the Waterloo corner. Beneath this sign, cut into the curved stone of the corner, was a memorial to Emma Cons, still visible today, bearing the not-very-inspired inscription: "Emma Cons, Founder of 'The Vic'. Alderman of the first London County Council. Born 1837 Died 1912. Lover of beauty and pupil of Ruskin. She yet gave [up] the life of an artist for social work, so deeply did she sympathize with those who lack many of the good things of life. To improve housing for working men and women, to provide wholesome and joyous recreation at low price, to promote education, to protect infant life, and bring a human touch to the children in the industrial schools of her day. To such beneficent ends she gave her very self, large-hearted and clear-sighted, courageous, tenacious of purpose and of great personal modesty. Her self-less appeal drew out the best in others and she was a constant inspiration for service to all with whom she was associated." In 1929 an additional monument to Emma Cons was unveiled, consisting of a large bas-relief portrait in the foyer. Near it was placed a portrait of King George V, "not quite so large as Aunt Emma's," Lilian Baylis once explained to Queen Mary, "because your dear husband has not done so much for the Old Vic."[22] In 1938 a new safety curtain was added, with a prize given for the most appropriate design. Painter Robert Morley won with a collection of iconic representations of the theatre's history and recent associations. At the left, as spectators, were Lilian Baylis standing beside a seated Emma Cons, and on stage were Hamlet with Yorick's skull, the clown from *Twelfth Night,* Oberon and Titania, a tree from Lear's heath, Bottom's ass's head, and some assiduous scene-shifters.

The heavy air raids during the fall of 1940 put an end to all theatrical activities in London, and this time the Vic was no exception. The theatre suffered no direct hits, but its roof was damaged, and this, with several years of desertion, made necessary another extensive refurbishing when it reopened in 1950. The continuing association with Shakespeare and the classic English tradition virtually guaranteed that the new audience-stage configuration would, so far as possible, reflect the most contemporary ideas on the staging of such works, and indeed the *Architect's Journal* of November 30, 1950, hailed the new stage as "the first large-scale attempt in this country to free the producer and the author from the limitations of the picture frame."[23] This 1950 arrangement was in fact a compromise between old and new ideas of stage structure. The proscenium was made extremely thick, extending well back into the stage space, with doors and balconies in its sides and the traditional stage curtain at its back. This created a large neutral area before the curtain which could serve as a traditional forestage, with a large proscenium stage behind. Decorative horizontal bands from the auditorium were carried onto the sides of this arch so that it would be tied visually to the house, rather than to the stage. Otherwise the arch was neutral except for the retention of the royal coat of arms above its center.

When the Old Vic became the official, if temporary, home of the National company in 1963 these ten-year-old redecorations were not considered sufficiently splendid, and the entire building was repainted and reupholstered. The forestage, already large, was now extended out into the house, covering the first two rows of seats, and within it was installed a large revolving stage. During all of these attempts to convert the stage area into the mid-twentieth-century ideal of a flexible and neutral space, the auditorium facing it remained essentially unchanged, creating an increasing disjuncture between these spaces.

Not long after the National left the Old Vic for its new South Bank location, the Old Vic was placed on sale and purchased by a Canadian entrepreneur, "Honest Ed" Mirvish, who, having restored the Edwardian Royal Theatre in Toronto to its nineteenth-century splendor, planned to undertake a similar project in London. Previous remodelings of the Vic had normally attempted, as is usual with theatre remodelings, to bring the structure more into line with contemporary spatial and decorative codes, and this new remodeling was no exception, though our contemporary codes include the conscious, if somewhat distorted, replication of earlier codes. The official history of the new theatre, *The Old Vic Refurbished,* speaks of its "restoration" to "its former Victorian splendor" and to "its nineteenth-century glory,"[24] although "splendor" and "glory" were certainly not terms applied to the building by observers in

the Victorian period. In fact the restoration has been rather more ac-
curately described by the *Stage Guardian* as a "curious mixture of magical
restoration and Disneyland pastiche."[25] Still, this sort of "curious mixture" is in fact an important part of contemporary public architecture,
as Disneyland overwhelmingly demonstrates.

"Mirvish is a great believer in signs," reported Sheridan Morley in a
London Times interview of June 21, 1983, and indeed for many months
in 1982–83 a great banner stretched along the scaffold-covered Waterloo
Road side of the closed theatre proclaimed, "Lilian Baylis—You're
Gonna Love This—Honest Ed." A less blatant use of signs is in fact
everywhere to be seen in the work Mirvish and his architects carried out
behind this scaffolding. The "refurbished" theatre is in fact an almost
new creation, but one which everywhere combines historical indices with
contemporary architectural and decorative codes. The facade has been
essentially rebuilt as a modified and Georgianized version of Cabanal's
rather plain original, crowned once more by a broken pediment, although now within the pediment are the lion, unicorn, and royal arms
of Victoria. This coat of arms, displayed during the nineteenth century
by the Old Vic as a sign suggesting official legitimacy never in fact
accorded the theatre, continues to serve a similar function today. Indeed, even the formal Royal Patent theatres—Drury Lane, Covent Garden, and Haymarket—are more sparing in their use of this sign than
the Vic, which uses it externally to crown its facade, internally to cap its
proscenium (in both locations it is accented by special spotlights), and
also on all programs, posters, letterheads, and official publications of the
theatre.

In the middle of the new facade, where Cabanal had placed "ROYAL
COBURG THEATRE" in incised letters, we now see "THE OLD VIC."
Cabanal's Waterloo Road and Webber Street sides, little changed by the
various remodelings, have now been incorporated more distinctly into
the visual statement of the building as a whole, since discreet lighting
picks out their brick arches at night, echoing the arches of the flood-
lighted facade. Mirvish had hoped to outline the building in lights, in
the manner of Harrods Department Store or the Victorian "reconstructions" of Disney World, but was prevented from doing so by city regulations concerning historic buildings.

The entrances of the facade are essentially those of the most recent
remodeling (1927), but over them is a porch with Tuscan columns, echoing the one added after a few years to Cabanal's original facade. Through
these doors one enters a lobby quite unlike anything in the theatre's
history—rather more, as some reviewers have remarked, like a contemporary luxury hotel, very large and light, with a minimum of specific
decoration. A broad, sweeping staircase at the left gives access to all upper
areas, a democratic idea unthinkable in a standard nineteenth-century
theatre. The changing codes of audience expectations are here clearly

evident. The carefully separated routes of public access, which gave to Victorian audiences a comfortable assurance of their class position, are characterized in the new official history of the theatre as a "dismal laby- rinth an audience was expected to negotiate." On the other hand, a careful attempt has been made to provide these major public areas, seeking spatially to send a message of modern comfort, even opulence, with indices of nineteenth-century elegance. Carpeting and wallpaper are designed from Victorian patterns, as are the globed chandeliers and the lines (though not the colors) of the huge window draperies. A large center ottoman of nineteenth-century design, with a potted palm, is placed in the center of the first-floor lobby. In the foyer on each level there is now a bar, following contemporary theatre practice. The upper ones are fairly featureless, but the one in the lower level, the "Pit Bar," with lower ceilings, tables, and darker colors, "recreates," according to its apologists, "the more intimate atmosphere of a Victorian 'Dive.' "[26]

The anomaly of creating such an area in the old Victoria Hall indi- cates clearly that the modern refurbishment is seeking to appeal to widely accepted public images of Victorian culture, rather than to the unique history of this structure. Nowhere is the disjuncture between the Vic's actual history and the modern "reconstruction" of that history more apparent than in the rear room of the Pit Bar, where the bronze plaque bearing Emma Cons' image (too dark and too heavy to be suitable for the new lobby) has been placed to watch over the modern patrons of her Temperance Music Hall enjoying their drinks from the bar between acts.

The words "refurbishment" and "restoration" are both frequently found in the literature of the new Old Vic, but historical elements and associations are everywhere used not for their original purposes, but as signs validating the Vic to contemporary audiences as a legitimate his- torical and cultural Victorian artifact. The passageways leading from the foyers to the auditorium are lined with pictures showing, on the first floor, the facades and interiors of the theatre at different periods, and on the second floor, famous actors who have performed there. The upper circle is now named for Lilian Baylis, and her photograph, with that of Emma Cons, hangs in the foyer there. Near them, in a rather obscure corner, stands the bust of Shakespeare, so long a major cultural icon in this theatre. The right and left stage boxes have been named for Laurence Olivier and Tyrone Guthrie, in memory of their association with this theatre, though the boxes themselves did not exist when they performed there (and indeed represented a feature of theatre which Guthrie in particular strongly opposed). Framed reproductions of nine- teenth-century playbills and other memorabilia line the walls of the Pit Bar. In the center of the main foyer, etched on a large mirror, is a reproduction of the famous looking-glass mirror of the Royal Coburg. Another large mirror, in the stairwell, bears at the bottom the names of the various architects who have supervised the various remodelings of the building.

The auditorium has been restored essentially to its physical appearance at its most ornate period, the 1880s, except that all areas now have comfortable and modern seats. The forestage and heavy proscenium added in the twentieth century have been replaced by a simpler Victorian frame, and even the four flags around the surmounting coat of arms have been restored, although these flags (made of fiberglass and painted to suggest great age) are now symbolic of the new orientation of the theatre—the Union Jack, the flag of Saint George, that of the Dominion of Canada, and that of Mirvish's hometown of Toronto. Sixty-three small diamonds of glass cover the new front curtain, supposedly to suggest the famous looking-glass curtain of an earlier era. Such self-conscious historical quotation has from time to time been utilized before in the Old Vic's history, but never in so pervasive a manner as in the modern remodeling. Yet never in the history of this venerable theatre has its surrounding culture been so encouraging of this sort of architectural nostalgia. The new Old Vic is far less the return to the architectural and decorative codes of previous eras which it at first appears to be than an expression of certain contemporary expectations and interests. It will, no doubt, as the *Stage Guardian* suggested soon after its opening, "be seen in future years as other remodelings of the past are seen today, as a metaphor for an age."[27]

NOTES

1. *The Builder*, 29 (December 30, 1871), 1029.
2. Richard Findlater, *Lilian Baylis* (London, 1975), 130.
3. Cecily Hamilton and Lilian Baylis, *The Old Vic* (London, 1926), 38.
4. John Booth, *The Old Vic* (London, 1917), 24.
5. Edward Walford, *Old and New London*, 4 vol. (London, 1887), 4:393.
6. Booth, *Vic*, 24.
7. Charles Dickens, *Sketches by Boz* (London, 1866), 51–52.
8. F. G. Tomlin, *Brief View of the English Drama* (London, 1840), 61.
9. *Penny Magazine* (1846), 167.
10. Charles Kingsley, *Alton Locke* (London, 1884), 117.
11. H. C. Newton, *The Old Vic and Its Associations* (London, 1923), 38.
12. Walford, *London*, 4:412.
13. W. F. E. C. Isaac, *Ben Greet and the Old Vic* (London, n.d.), 38.
14. John Elsom and Nicholas Tomalin, *The History of the National Theatre* (London, 1978), 82.
15. Eric Bentley, *The Life of the Drama* (New York, 1964), 43.
16. Edwin Fagg, *The Old "Old Vic"* (London, 1936), 31.
17. Booth, *Vic*, 20.

18. E. W. Brayley, *Historical and Descriptive Accounts of the Theatres of London* (London, 1826), 20.

19. John Hollinshead, *Ragged Life in London* (London, 1861), 180.

20. Hamilton and Baylis, *Vic,* 206.

21. Hamilton and Baylis, *Vic,* 211.

22. Harcourt Williams, *Old Vic Saga* (London, 1949), 23.

23. *The Architect's Journal* (Nov. 30, 1950), 41.

24. D. F. Cheshire, Sean McCarthy, and Hilary Norris, *The Old Vic Refurbished* (London, 1983), 34.

25. *Stage Guardian* (Nov. 4, 1983), 11.

26. Cheshire, et al., *Vic,* 36.

27. *Stage Guardian* (Nov. 4, 1983), 11.

✷ ✷ ✷ ✷ ✷   The Iconic Stage

SEMIOTIC ANALYSES OF theatre have often given particular emphasis to the extreme importance in this art of a particular type of sign: the icon. According to C. S. Peirce, who established this as a key semiotic term, "anything whatever, be it quality, existent individual, or law, is an Icon of anything, in so far as it is like that thing and used as a sign of it."[1] The theatre more than any other art deals in things that are like other things, offering, in the words of Peter Handke, light which is brightness pretending to be another brightness, a chair pretending to be another chair, and so on.[2] Nevertheless, this ability, one might even say this tendency, of theatre to invest pieces of reality with its particular artistic significations is not only a distinguishing feature of this art, but also, as Bert States has argued in a fascinating essay on this subject, a source of particular artistic power.[3]

In every historical period there has been an interplay between iconic and other types of sign presentation on stage, but different periods and different traditions have varied greatly both in the degree of iconicity on stage and in the relationship between the icon and its referent. Indeed, the stylistic differences between different theatrical traditions may often be described in terms of their differences in iconicity. The Western realistic tradition is of course highly iconic. Indeed, one might define theatrical realism as an attempt to create as iconic a performance as the medium will allow. The costumes the actors wear, the properties they manipulate, the furniture they use are carefully selected or created to approximate such objects in the world outside the theatre as closely as possible. In more stylized theatres, most notably those of the classic Orient, symbolization often replaces iconicity—a table represents a mountain; a flag, an army; a piece of cloth, a river.

Although one might say that realism is a style in which everything on stage is presented as an icon, a distinction could nevertheless be made between different types of iconic representation within a realistic production. Although theatre theorists tend to think of icons in Handke's terms ("chairs pretending to be other chairs"), Peirce's definition is much more general, requiring only that the icon be "like that thing" it stands for. Thus a chair painted on a canvas backdrop (a common sight in prerealistic theatre) would be as legitimate an icon as a real chair, one of States' "pieces of reality" appropriated by the theatre for its own purposes. We might thus make a distinction between the general iconic feature of similarity and the common situation in theatre where objects actually *are* the things they represent, a situation to which Kier Elam has given the name *iconic identity*.[4]

In any theatre, even when it is highly realistic, the degree of iconic identity of different elements will vary. The one element which almost invariably involves iconic identity, no matter how stylized the production, is the actor, a human being who represents a human being. The most notable exceptions to this, shadow or puppet plays, are generally considered distinct and separate subgenres of theatre. Predictably, iconic identity on stage is next most commonly found in those elements most closely associated with and most utilized by the actor: the crown he wears, the fan she carries, the furnishings they sit upon. In realistic drama, both contemporary and historical, the iconic identity of such items is of major importance and on occasion has exceeded even the normal idea of iconic identity. Sometimes for purposes of publicity, sometimes for a more disinterested motive of artistic verisimilitude, directors and designers have placed on stage objects which did not simply resemble real-life objects, but were in fact the objects themselves—actual contemporary or period costumes or furniture, borrowed from homes or museums; real flowers on real tables; real food really eaten; even, when it could be afforded, real gold and jewelry on the leading ladies.

The stage element which historically has most resisted representation through iconic identity, even during the realistic era, has been the physical setting, the scenery (as opposed to properties). There are obvious practical reasons for this. Clearly, the presentation of a real Louis XIV chair, or a real pearl necklace, or a even a real horse presents far fewer problems than a real town square, a real forest, or even a real architectural interior. The interiors were of course what the realistic theatre favored, but in fact they were constructed the same way that town squares or forests were—from wooden frames, canvas, and paint. The doors and the pictures on the walls might be real, and great care might be taken to ensure that the walls did not sway when doors were vigorously slammed, but the walls were not real walls, and the room was not a real room in the same way that the chairs were real chairs. The scenery was iconic in Peirce's general sense, but it did not participate in iconic identity.

Nor was this necessarily a shortcoming, even for the most doctrinaire of realists. Clearly, a certain pleasure of theatre placing great stress on verisimilitude is appreciation of the art required to create this impression. When Belasco recreated the interior of a Child's restaurant on stage, the fascination of the audience was obviously not in seeing in total and authentic detail the interior of such a restaurant. They could, of course, walk into any restaurant in this popular chain without paying admission and have that experience. The fascination was in seeing this familiar scene recreated on stage with an indistinguishable blend of an iconic setting and properties which might be either iconic or actually be the objects represented. Part of the pleasure involved here is simply that of appreciation of the technical skill of the scenic artist, seemingly overcoming the particular intractability of theatrical scenery to the sort of iconic identity so common in other aspects of theatre production. But there is also a more complex audience response at work.

In his famous essay on psychical distance early in this century, Edward Bullough gave particular attention to theatre. Briefly, it is Bullough's contention that an apprehension of Distance is necessary to appreciate any work of art, indeed even to experience it *as* art. This apprehension may be lost if the Distance becomes too great or too small, and the theatre runs a particular risk of the latter, "owing to the material presentment of its subject matter,"[5] in other words, to its strong reliance upon iconic identity. At the same time, Bullough recognizes that particular satisfaction can be attained from this decrease of Distance, provided that it remains controlled: "both in appreciation and in production, most desirable is the utmost decrease of Distance without its disappearance."[6] Even when nothing on the stage itself served to distance the audience from the reality of Belasco's setting, the fact that it *was* on a stage, displayed—or, in Eco's useful term, *ostended*—for its public's contemplation, provided precisely the minimum distancing Bullough demanded, and created an agreeable tension between the audience's knowledge of illusion and its appreciation of the illusion's effectiveness. However complete the stage illusion, the audience necessarily remains aware of it *as* illusion. They are aware intellectually that beyond the plate-glass windows of Belasco's restaurant setting is not a New York street, but the back wall of the stage, and even more directly, they are aware physically that they are sitting in a theatre auditorium as members of an observing audience.

The production tradition that reached its high point in such masters of detailed iconic representation as Belasco is generally styled realistic and is obviously reinforced by the bourgeois interest in authenticating realistic detail and material culture, but romanticism also contributed in an important manner to this tradition, anticipating the attention of the realists to the exact reproduction of all aspects of contemporary life by carefully researched reconstructions of historical scenes and dedication to local color. Perhaps nowhere was this romantic/realistic devotion to iconic production more striking or more challenging to theatrical resources than in the nineteenth-century tradition of production of Shakespeare.

In an actual Elizabethan performance, of course, a street scene, a forest, or a chamber would have been as far from any iconic representation of the original as the neutral settings of the French classic stage, but now Shakespeare began to be presented according to the new vision of the historically accurate setting. During the late nineteenth and early twentieth centuries this became the main line of Shakespearian interpretation, exemplified by such major directors as Kean, Irving, and Beerbohm-Tree in England, Daly and Booth in America, the Duke of Saxe-Meiningen in Germany, and Antoine in France.

The logistics of presenting multiscene plays like those of Shakespeare within detailed iconic settings proved formidable indeed, straining the resources of Europe's largest and best-equipped theatres and the imaginations of the finest engineers and designers, aided by all manner of revolving, sliding, and elevating stage areas. Few directors since the early years of the twentieth century have attempted to return to the sort of stage filled with authentic bushes and rabbits which was a specialty of Beerbohm-Tree, although an occasional production has attracted attention as a novelty by showing unusual concern in this direction. The graphic decadence of the 1933 New York production of *Tobacco Road* (earning it a highly unusual run of more than seven years) was emphasized by the real dirt, weeds, and filth which covered the stage. Audiences and critics were so fascinated by the detailed duplication of a tenement facade on a New York stage of Elmer Rice's *Street Scene* and by the more recent creation of the side of a mountain for Patrick Meyers' *K2* that these settings dominated both contemporary reactions to these productions and the memories of them.

Despite a few such striking exceptions, detailed illusionistic settings of this sort have rarely been seen in the modern theatre, partly in reaction to the turn-of-the-century excesses in such productions, and partly due to a feeling that such displays distracted from other and more important values of the dramatic work. Perhaps the major reason, however, has been that the evolving cinema offered a far more effective way of placing before the viewer's gaze any location in the world as desired, without the problems of shifting stage scenery. The gain in flexibility and accuracy of scenic detail was considerable, even though an important sacrifice was also involved—the phenomenological essence of theatre, its physical presence. Cinema as an art is as heavily iconic as theatre, but the theatre's shifting mixture of iconicity is necessarily absent in film. There can be no physical iconic identity of actors or objects. All icons become the same—projected images of absent realities. Christian Metz makes this point clearly in "The Imaginary Signifier":

> The perceptions that theatre and other spectacles offer to the eye and ear are inscribed in a true space (not a photographed one), the same one as that occupied by the public during the performance; everything the audience hear and see is actively produced in their presence, by human beings or props which are themselves present. This is not the problem of fiction but that of the definitional characteristics of the signifier: whether or not the theatrical play mimes a fable, its *action,* if need be mimetic, is still managed by real persons evolving in real time and space, *on the same stage or "scene" as the public.* The "other scene," which is precisely not so called, is the cinematic screen (closer to fantasy from the outset): what unfolds there may, as before, be more or less fiction, but the unfolding itself is fictive: the actors, the "decor," the words one hears are all absent, everything is *recorded* (as a memory trace which is immediately so, without having been something else before), and this is still true if what is recorded is not a "story" and does not aim for the fictional illusion proper. For it is the signifier itself, and as a whole, that is recorded, that is absence.[7]

Metz's observation, perceptive as it is, still requires a certain qualification. Certainly, as compared with the cinema, it is true to say that public and performance in theatre occupy the same "true space," but in terms of reception it is equally important to remember that, normally speaking, audience and performance do not in fact occupy the same space, but two contiguous spaces simultaneously, the space of the viewer and the space of the viewed. In almost every period of theatre history the disjuncture between these spaces has been emphasized by physical means, and often by actual barriers—most commonly the raising of the actor's space above that of the audience, but also by the use of curtains, proscenium arches and frames, by the "mystic abyss" of the Wagnerian orchestra pit, by all sorts of railings and balustrades, and so on. As André Bazin has observed, theatre "of its very essence must not be confused with nature under penalty of being absorbed by her and ceasing to be," and to protect this essential division, the architecture of the stage "has varied from time to time without ever ceasing to mark out a privileged spot actually or virtually distinct from nature."[8] Although Bullough stresses that the Distance he is considering is mental rather than physical, he does remark that actual spatial distance, especially in an art such as theatre, contributes to the mental process which interests him. He even goes so far as to suggest that "the actual *spatial distance* separating objects of sight and hearing from the subject" has been one of the major reasons why the arts appealing to the ear and eye have been developed in a way that potential gustatory, olfactory, or haptic arts have not.[9]

The theatre, as a particularly tangible art, has always drawn an important part of its power from its physical presence even when actors and audiences were spatially separated. During the twentieth century, when the emergence of film has by contrast called particular attention to this quality of theatre, we have seen an unusually rich variety of productions which in fact brought actors and audience into the "same space." One may call this, as Metz does, the same "true" space, to distinguish it from the photographed space of the film; but "true" is a potentially misleading word here, since space, like any other "true" reality, can be readily iconicized by the theatre. Actors may certainly share the same "true" space as their public, even capitalizing upon those sensory connections deprecated by Bullough, as when the Bread and Puppet company comes into the audience to share food with the spectators, or when Peter Brook's *Midsummer Night's Dream* company left the stage to clasp hands with the public.

Actor and audience spaces may be shared in a quite different way, however, if the actors do not invade the audience's space but require the audience to enter the iconic space of the performance. Two important pioneers in such experiments were Max Reinhardt and Nikolai Oklopkov. For one of his most famous productions, *The Miracle,* Reinhardt in the 1920s converted the entire interiors of theatres in several cities, such as the Century in New York, into vast Gothic cathedrals, with the audience seated in the nave. In the 1930s Oklopkov in Moscow converted the entire interior of his theatre into a hillside, where the audience sat among the actors as if "encamped with the Red Army in the field."[10] In such productions, audiences most often are accepted by the actors as nonspeaking sharers of the iconic space.

More recent interest in such experimentation doubtless owes much to the work in the early 1960s of the extremely influential Polish director Jerzy Grotowski, who followed Oklopkov in mixing actor and audience spaces in different ways for different productions. For *Kordian,* his small theatre became a mental hospital with beds for both actors and audience, and for *Dr. Faustus,* the audience was seated at two long refectory tables as guests at Faustus' final banquet. In America, performances of this sort were sometimes called "environmental," a term first applied to a 1967 production of Ionesco's *Victims of Duty* at the Petit Théâtre du Vieux Carré in New Orleans, where the entire auditorium and stage was converted into a living room inhabited by both actors and audience.[11] As Reinhardt and Oklopkov demonstrated, either interior or exterior space may be treated in this manner. When Peter Stein produced Shakespeare's *As You Like It* in 1977 he did not, as Irving or Daly would have done, create an iconic woodland on stage inaccessible to the audience, but brought the audience into a space which they shared with actors, a space containing a pond, a field of corn, and real trees, with birdcalls coming from all sides.[12]

In each of these examples, the introduction of the audience into the illusory iconic space of the production emphasizes in a powerful way the tangible reality, the "thingness" of the theatre, especially in contrast to a medium such as film, but the iconic space itself is not essentially different from that of nineteenth-century realism. The pond and trees may be real, but Stein's woodland itself is not (even the birds are recorded). The furnishings in *Victims of Duty* may be real, but the living room itself is not. In short, such productions still follow the normal practice of nineteenth-century realism, utilizing iconic identity for actors, costumes, and properties placed within an illusionistic setting. From the point of view of the audience, there is no question that either bringing actors into the public space or bringing the public into the iconic space of the performance will almost certainly bring about an important diminishing of both spatial and psychical distance, with the result that audience members may suffer the disturbance of underdistancing. That this does not happen more often is surely because the performance event still provides its own distancing through the audience's viewing of it as such an event. The proscenium arch and the familiar auditorium may have disappeared, but in each of the productions just mentioned, the audience came to a familiar structure, a theatre building, within which they were accustomed to finding prepared illusions. Even when the performance sought to absorb the audience in its own iconic space, the spectactors remained aware that that space was in turn abosrbed within the overarching space of the theatre building itself, which both contained and legitimitized this illusory world.

A more radical spatial organization occurs when this sheltering structure is given up entirely or in part and the audience is asked to relate in some manner to real external space. In an interesting early experiment in this direction, Goethe assembled the Weimar court one evening in a small outdoor pavilion on the royal estate. The back wall had been removed, and the audience was seated facing it as if it were a proscenium opening. What the audience observed was a wooded glade and the bend of a stream. Under these circumstances, a boat coming down the stream with lanterns and a singing oarsman seemed quite magical, as did such effects as the bobbing of other lanterns carried by actors through the woods.[13] Unlike the garden theatres of the baroque period, which sought to impose the artificiality of the theatrical imagination upon nature,

Goethe's *Muses' Cottage* utilized nature for an authenticity impossible to achieve in a theatre setting.

As an interest in theatrical iconicity increased along with the growing taste for realism during the nineteenth century, the particular difficulty of representing iconic exterior scenes on a conventional stage encouraged a number of producers to offer plays as Goethe did, in actual woods and meadows. One of the first groups in England to offer such productions, the Pastoral Players, presented scenes from *As You Like It* and Fletcher's *The Faithful Shepherdesse* in the Coombe Woods in 1884–85. The resulting comments from *Era* magazine make clear the appeal of these experiments: "Not only did the mounting leave nothing to the imagination, more even than imitating reality with photographic accuracy, it was reality itself."[14] In the opening years of the twentieth century, open-air theatres offering "reality itself" enjoyed a great vogue in Europe and America. Probably the most famous of these was the German Harzer Bergtheater, founded in 1903 for the production of dramas drawn from Teutonic mythology but in fact most successful in the performance of *A Midsummer Night's Dream*.

A very different reception dynamic is involved in the apparently very similar Peter Stein and Pastoral Players presentations of *As You Like It*, both bringing their audiences into direct contact with real natural objects, and this reception dynamic results from the difference between the simple iconicity of Stein's actual performance *space* (a theatre interior which resembled a real exterior space) and the iconic identity of the Pastoral Players' space (an actual woods ulitized as a woods). In simple iconicity, the professed aim may be to encourage the audience to forget that it is in a theatre, but in fact the more detailed and accurate the reproduction of external reality is, the more likely that an important part of the audience's reaction to (and pleasure with) the production will involve a sense of wonder at the authenticity of the illusion. An important element of almost every review of Reinhardt's *The Miracle* was the wonder the audience felt at the seeming conversion of a theatrical space into a Gothic interior. Typical was the reaction of *The New York Times,* which, under the headline "Scenic Miracle Wrought," assured its audiences that what they would experience at the Century Theatre was "not a mere contrivance of canvas and paint, but a solid structure of wood and iron and concrete and seeming stone."[15] As we have noted, similar reactions greeted the productions in later years of *Tobacco Road, Street Scene,* and *K2.*

When the drama moves out of the theatre into iconic settings such as the Coombe Woods, a quite different audience reaction may be observed. Had Reinhardt carried out his plans to produce *The Miracle* in Milan Cathedral, one would hardly have expected any audience member to find any fascination in how much this interior resembled an actual cathedral. The source of pleasure here is of a quite different sort, in a certain sense almost a reversal of the source within the theatre. In the theatre, one might say, we see illusion and amuse ourselves by pretending it is reality, while in the Coombe Woods we see reality and amuse ourselves by pretending it is theatre.

It is only by such pretending that we can maintain in the Coombe Woods the distance from reality that makes theatre reception possible at all. Two centuries after Goethe's entertainment, Bruce Wilshire's report on *Light Touch* in New York described the effect of a similar experiment, with an open warehouse door revealing an urban rather than a bucolic external world. The normally banal spectacle of passing traffic was converted into something strange and fascinating.

> . . . cars appeared occasionally, framed by the door, as they passed on the street directly outside. Appeared, but appeared transfigured, as if a spell had been cast over them. Details of their shape and movement, ordinarily not noticed, leapt out, as if from a numinous aura. It was as if cars were being seen for the first time.[16]

Clearly, the theatrical "frame" provided by the open door and the traditional separation of the seated public from the "scene" within this frame serve to stimulate in the audience the feeling that it is watching not reality, but theatre, and everything observed becomes infused with iconicity. Once again we see that although distancing occurs in the mind, in situations where theatre and reality come dangerously close, some specific spatial framing device may be employed to prevent misinterpretation.

I should like to consider one further refinement of iconic space which has long provided an important and rather different variation both on the theatre experience and on the means by which distance is achieved. Iconic space was, as I have already observed, a particular concern of many romantic dramatists. Victor Hugo championed the use of such iconicity in his opposition to the traditional neoclassic unities, arguing that unity of place forced the dramatist to falsify his action by placing it in incorrect settings:

> Exact locality is one of the first elements of reality. The speaking or acting characters alone do not engrave on the soul of the spectator the faithful impression of facts. The place where such a catastrophe occurred becomes a terrible and inseparable witness of it, and the absence of this sort of silent character makes the greatest scenes of history in the drama incomplete. Would the poet dare to assassinate Rizzo elsewhere than in Mary Stuart's chamber? stab Henri IV elsewhere than in that rue de la Ferronier, obstructed with drays and carriages? burn Joan of Arc elsewhere than in the old market-place?[17]

For the romantics, this line of argument supported what seemed to be the practice of Shakespeare, placing each scene in its proper setting, as opposed to Racine, with his famous single neutral chamber. Clearly, when Hugo asserts that the poet must assassinate Rizzo in Mary Stuart's chamber and burn Joan of Arc in the old marketplace, he is insisting that scenes in the theatre must shift iconically to these locations instead of relying upon the neutral spaces of the French classic stage. One might take his advice literally, however, performing a dramatization of these events in their actual historical locations instead of on stage, or in a setting like the Coombe Woods or the Harz Mountains which is "real," but which is not in fact the actual location of the play's action. The Tell-Spiele, organized in 1912 at Interlaken in Switzerland, for example, performed Schiller's epic drama in a small village and wood setting against an Alpine background which was offered, with a certain stretch of the imagination, as the authentic location for at least some of the scenes of the play.

To take a more recent example, a very popular production of the 1980s has been John Krizanc's *Tamara*, offered first in Toronto and subsequently in Los Angeles and New York. For this production, ten large rooms with connecting halls and staircases must be found in an available building (in New York, the Park Avenue Armory). These are furnished to represent Il Vittoriale, the country villa of Gabriele d'Annunzio, in 1927, and audience members are allowed to follow any one of the play's characters through these rooms during the evening, thus experiencing only that part of the total action in which that character is involved (the play's producers call it a "living movie"). Here walls, staircases, windows, and rooms are represented by real walls, staircases, windows, and rooms, not by painted canvas; but one could imagine another performance of the same work actually staged in the villa of Il Vittoriale, where the physical surroundings could authentically fulfill Hugo's role of silent witnesses to these events.

"Iconic identity," seemingly a fairly precise concept, does not allow us to make this distinction, which is of considerable importance in reception. Just as we have distinguished already between simple iconicity (a flat scenic element cut and painted to resemble a tree) and iconic identity (an actual tree appearing in a signifying context), I would like to further distinguish between general iconic identity (a real forest representing a forest in a play) and specific iconic identity (the actual forest mentioned in the script, if it exists, being utilized as a setting for that play). Although general iconic identity is what we normally encounter in theatre, there is no element of theatre which has not at one time or another utilized specific iconic identity as well. The actor, the theatrical element most closely involved with general iconic identity, is perhaps the element least likely to utilize specific iconic identity, since the "playing" of someone "other" seems to lie at the very basis of theatre. Nevertheless, the history of the theatre offers many examples of actors appearing as icons of themselves. The experimental tradition of the twentieth century, from Pirandello to the Living Theatre, has often employed this strategy (Robert Brustein's 1988 production of Pirandello's *Six Characters* emphasized this by having the actors play themselves), but it is by no means a development tied to the contemporary passion for self-reflexivity. Adam de la Halle appeared as the central character in his own play, the fascinating late medieval *Jeu de la feuillée,* and Molière and his fellows appeared as icons of themselves in his *Impromptu de Versailles.* Nor is this phenomenon only a product of artistic self-conciousness or experimentation; quite striking examples may be found in less literary or artistic sources. Late-nineteenth-century variety entertainments often featured famous or notorious persons who did not perform, but merely appeared to expose themselves to the public gaze. In a more traditional theatrical context appeared William F. Cody, playing himself in countless spectacles of daring deeds in the old West. Robert Darnton analyses a fascinating example of this phenomenon in an improvised entertainment among printers' apprentices in Paris in the 1730s.[18]

Performance spaces with specific iconic identity relate to their audiences in quite different ways than do other types of iconic stages. In literal examples of Hugo's physical locations which have been "silent characters" in historical events, the audience's contact with such locations seems to provide a measure of contact with the reality of the events themselves. The earliest known examples of theatrical activity were all in sites with rich historical and religious meanings. Every faith has established holy places with real or legendary associations to the great events in its development, and there is often a close connection between these observances, especially if they have a dramatic element, and the legendary or mythical events which contributed to the sanctification of this place. Abydos in Egypt, a pilgrimage site for nearly three thousand years, offered mystery plays dealing with the story of Osiris upon the very island which was honored as his place of burial.[19]

Quasitheatrical performances were also found to have been presented from a very early date at the Christian shrines in Jerusalem. The most detailed report of an early pilgrimage is that of Egeria in 381–84. At such locations as the Upper Room, the Mount of Olives, and Golgotha, the faithful gathered on appropriate days to hear the gospel account of events in those places read. The recurring phrase "on the same day in the very place" indicates the importance of the setting to Egeria's experience. Some ceremonies came especially close to dramatic representation, such as the bishop's reading the news of the Resurrection to the congregation assembled before the tomb where the angel had presented the same words to the three Marys, or the Palm Sunday procession, where pilgrims and townspeople welcomed the bishop into the city with palm branches and songs of "Blessed is he who comes in the name of the Lord."[20]

The re-enactment of religious scenes on the sites of their presumed original occurrence is still found in the contemporary world, in traditional sites in the Holy Land and in new pilgrimage locations such as Hill Cumorah in upstate New York, where since 1937 the Mormon church has presented a huge outdoor pageant on the site where Joseph Smith is said to have found the tablets establishing the Mormon faith. For many spectators attendance at such spectacles may still provide something of the religious experience felt by medieval pilgrims like Egeria, but in this more secular world, a portion of the spectators may be expected to bring a primarily historical rather than religious interest to such re-creations. In many respects the modern tourist may be considered the direct descendent of the medieval pilgrim, and for both, the desire to visit the place where important events actually occurred has encouraged the development of dramatic or quasidramatic activities in those places reinforcing their historical "reality."

The Swiss Tell-Spiele may be taken as an early example of the historical drama, frequently performed in an outdoor theatre, which can now be found in many locations in the United States. *The Lost Colony,* begun in 1937 in Manteo, North Carolina, and *The Common Glory,* begun in 1947 in Williamsburg, Virginia, were early examples of a kind of celebration of local history which has since been offered in dozens of locations, many repeating these performances every year. In a variation of that type of performance, the sound-and-light show, the setting is no longer a silent character, but, with the aid of modern electronics, the principal—indeed, the sole—theatrical performer. Audiences seated before such monuments as the Acropolis, the Pyramids, or the Palace of Versailles witness a dramatization of the history of that setting, recounted by taped music and sound, and accompanied by lighting changes on the monument.

The actual re-creation of historical events on the site of their occurrence has been a widespread activity during the twentieth century. The post-Revolutionary Russian theatre, probably under the influence of the great national festivals of the French Revolution, undertook such stagings on a scale never before attempted. The most famous and spectacular of these was *The Taking of the Winter Palace* on November 7, 1920, a dramatic re-enactment of that major Revolutionary event, involving more than eight thousand participants. The director, Nikolai Evreinov, laid much stress on the fact that this work was "performed in the *actual place* where the historic event occurred."[21] A peak in such activities came in the United States between 1961 and 1965, during the centennial of the Civil War, and in 1975–76, the bicentennial of the Revolution. Countless battles and other historical events were re-created in their original locations, with actors in authentic costumes attempting to follow with varying exactness the actions of a century or two before. The re-creations ranged from major battles such as Gettysburg, Antietam, and Bull Run to more modest events such as Washington's crossing the Delaware, the inauguration of Jefferson Davis, Paul Revere's ride, Anthony Wayne's cattle drive to relieve the troops at Valley Forge, Grant's homecoming to Galena, Illinois, and Lincoln's address to the New Jersey legislature in 1861. Organizations such as the New York-based Brigade of the American Revolution provided historical advice, skilled performers, and authentic costumes to groups in many communities wishing to stage a local battle. In all of these re-creations, the boundary between theatre and reality is reinforced not spatially, as is traditionally the case, but temporally. The settings are taken to represent themselves at an earlier point in time.

As twentieth-century historians have become increasingly interested in the history of the hitherto often neglected lower classes, theatre practitioners have also sought to give a voice to such subjects, and this has resulted in some specific iconic stagings not at the scenes of great battles or of the deeds of famous leaders, but in the living and working places of the people. Armand Gatti, a pioneer in such experimentation, discovered in creating a play about a factory worker that the authentic milieu was as important to this common laborer as Hugo felt it was to the proper depiction of kings and saints. Observed Gatti:

> With this kind of subject it's mostly the *place,* the architecture that does the writing. The theatre was located not in some kind of Utopian place, but in a historic place, a place with a history. There was grease, and there were acid marks, because it was a chemical factory; you could still see traces of work; there were still work-clothes around; there were still lunch-pails in the corner, etc. In other words, all these left-over traces of work had their own language. These rooms that had known the labor of human beings day after day had their own language, and you either used that language or you didn't say anything. . . . That's why I wrote in an article "a play authored by a factory."[22]

Gatti has realized that Hugo's "silent character" may be silent in regard to spoken language, but that a vast number of other communications are provided by physical surroundings.

Most of the scripts for performances in historic spaces, with actors and without, have been created specifically for such performances, woven out of interesting material from local history. Occasionally, though, as with the Swiss *Tell* play, performances of already existing literary works have been offered in the actual or presumed sites of their action. In 1934 Reinhardt presented *The Merchant of Venice* in a Venetian square, the Campo San Trovaso, which contained a small bridge under which real gondolas passed and a picturesque house which, according to Reinhardt's research, had actually been the dwelling of a Venetian merchant in the sixteenth century. Three years later the Danish Tourist Board began sponsoring summer productions of *Hamlet* at Elsinore Castle, featuring such leading English theatre artists as Olivier, Guthrie, and Gielgud. For a number of years, beginning in 1962, *The Miracle Worker*, based on the life of Helen Keller, was produced on the lawn in front of her birthplace. Verdi's *Aida* has been performed in Luxor, and his *Nabucco*, before the ruins of Babylon. The best-known production of the Vermont Ensemble Theatre, an "environmental theatre" company organized in 1984, was their production of Wilder's *Our Town*, with different acts presented in different locations around the village green of Wilderesque Middlebury, Vermont, and with staged outdoor vignettes of village life presented to the spectators as they strolled by lantern light from one location to another.[23] Some communities offer, instead of formal dramatic presentations, more elaborate versions of the Middlebury vignettes, converting historic locations into a kind of living stage setting, where tourists may wander through period rooms or among period buildings, observing inhabitants dressed in historical costumes performing activities of a bygone era.

Since theatres also are structures with an historical dimension, they, too, have been used as icons of their historic selves. The best-known example of this is Drottningholm theatre in Sweden, a perfectly preserved eighteenth-century court theatre which offers to summer tourists performances of eighteenth-century opera staged according to the practices of that period, with even the orchestra members and the ushers wigged and costumed to give the visitor the sensation of having stepped into an eighteenth-century performance situation.

At Drottningholm, as in the case of every other example of specific iconic identity so far cited, the setting has been selected for its own specific involvement, real or imagined, in some historic event or period with which the spectator is to be brought into closer imaginative contact. In semiotic terms, the power of this sort of icon arises from the fact that it is also an index, pointing to the absent and distanced historic reality which interests the spectator. Obviously, this is often the case with specific iconic settings, but it is not necessarily so. In situations where the theatre itself has been used as a setting with specific iconic identity, as it has in almost every historical period, it has normally not served also as an index of an earlier historical period, but has represented itself in the present moment. Among the examples of such works we might cite Beaumont and Fletcher's *Knight of the Burning Pestle*, Rotrou's *Saint Genêt*, Molière's *Impromptu de Versailles*, Buckingham's *The Rehearsal*, Sheridan's *The Critic*, and Pirandello's *Six Characters in Search of an Author* or *Tonight We Improvise*. Since in such works the stage represents itself, not infrequently the characters appearing there also represent themselves, as we have already noted in the case of the *Impromptu* and of the modern Brustein production of *Six Characters*.

Although nontheatrical settings using specific iconic identity have often been historically oriented, they may also, like these theatrical examples, simply represent themselves as they presently exist. The already-mentioned *Jeu de la feuillée* stands as an isolated example from the late Middle Ages of a play whose setting is in fact the real area in which it was staged, the marketplace of the town of Arras. Renaissance court masques and similar entertainments often featured the mingling of performers and observers in a common space. In our own times, perhaps the most striking examples of specific iconic identity without the distancing effect of historical reference is in the work of performance artists, who may be said to have led their audiences through the warehouse door described by Wilshire into the real world beyond. *The Drama Review*, with its strong interest in nontraditional performance, has provided the best documentation of this development, with articles on such performance artists as Jamie Leo, who has utilized his own apartment for staged events; Danny Mydlack, who organizes shows in homes in Boston; and Anne Bogart, who guides her audiences on "performance journeys" through the streets of New York.[24]

Most of these events have a social or political dimension, but their major effect is to "theatricalize" locations in the real world, and their success demonstrates that the distancing essential to the theatrical experience can be attained even without any of the traditional devices. All that is necessary is that the audience decide, as a matter of choice, to view the world about it "theatrically," a choice traditionally encouraged by such devices as framing or ostending. Aesthetician Roger Scruton, drawing upon Wittgenstein's useful distinction between "seeing" and "seeing as," states that in ordinary perception our belief in what we are "seeing" is involuntary, but in imaginative states we *will* ourselves to "see as," without the necessity of belief,[25] a modern reformulation of that imaginative process which was a central concern of the romantics and which Coleridge most famously articulated as the "willing suspension of disbelief."

As theatre, in its continuing colonization of reality, has moved outside its traditional spaces and renounced the conventional "frames" of elevated stage or encompassing proscenium, the importance of "seeing as" has become especially clear, as has the close relationship between this process and the role of the icon in the theatrical experience. The conversion of real space into iconic space, a conversion essential for it to be utilized in theatre, depends precisely upon a person or, more commonly, a group of people choosing not merely to "see" it, but to "see it as," in Wittgenstein's terms. This is what occurs when, as Bullough observes, "by a sudden change of inward perspective, we are overcome by the feeling that 'all the world's a stage.' "[26] Although the practice of traditional theatre would lead us to expect, as even the more experimental examples in this discussion have illustrated, that the process of iconization is suggested and stimulated in the public by external "creators" of the event, it is clear that the audience itself could create such an experience. Such an activity was in fact suggested in the writings of the early Evreinov, who, a decade before he became involved with such specific iconizations of historical space as *The Taking of the Winter Palace,* encouraged his readers to create theatre out of everyday life by viewing reality in this way.[27] When Evreinov called for a theatricaliation of the world, he could as well be said to be calling for the iconization of it.

NOTES

1. C. S. Peirce, *Collected Papers* (Cambridge, Mass., 1931–58), vol. 2, par. 247.

2. Peter Handke, *Kaspar and Other Plays,* trans. Michael Roloff (New York, 1969), 10.

3. Bert O. States, "The World on Stage," in *Great Reckonings in Little Rooms: On the Phenomonology of Theatre* (Berkeley, 1985), 19–47.

4. Kier Elam, *The Semiotics of Theatre and Drama* (London, 1980), 22–23.

5. Edward Bullough, " 'Psychical Distance' as a Factor in Art and an Aesthetic Principle," *British Journal of Psychology* 5 (June 1912), 97.

6. Bullough, "Psychical Distance," 94.

7. Christian Metz, "The Imaginary Signifier," trans. Ben Brewster, *Screen* 16 (Summer 1975), 21.

8. André Bazin, "Theatre and Cinema," in *What Is Cinema?,* vol. 1, trans. Hugh Gray (Berkeley, 1967), 140.

9. Bullough, "Psychical Distance," 96.

10. Norris Houghton, *Moscow Rehearsals* (New York, 1936), 23.

11. Brooks McNamara, Jerry Rojo, Richard Schechner, *Theatres, Spaces, Environments* (New York, 1975), 2.

12. Michael Patterson, *Peter Stein* (Cambridge, 1981), 139.

13. Gisela Sichardt, *Das Weimarer Liebhabertheater unter Goethes Leitung* (Weimar, 1957), 62–64.

14. *Era,* June 6, 1885.

15. *New York Times,* January 16, 1924, 17.

16. Bruce Wilshire, *Role Playing and Identity* (Bloomington, 1982), x.

17. Victor Hugo, *Oeuvres complètes,* 18 v. (Paris, 1967), 3:63.

18. Robert Darnton, *The Great Cat Massacre* (New York, 1985).

19. R. T. R. Clark, *Myth and Symbol in Ancient Egypt* (London, 1959), 65.

20. E. D. Hunt, *Holy Land Pilgrimage in the Later Roman Empire, A. D. 312–460* (Oxford, 1982), 112–16, 123.

21. Nikolai Evreinov, *Histoire du théâtre russe,* trans. G. Welter (Paris, 1947), 146–47.

22. Armand Gatti, "Armand Gatti on Time, Place, and the Theatrical Event," trans. Nancy Oakes, *Modern Drama,* 25:1 (March 1982), 71–72.

23. Leslie Bennetts, "Staging 'La Strada' in a Vermont Field Requires Invention," *New York Times,* July 21, 1987, C13:1. For more information on the history and practices of American outdoor historical drama, see George MacCalmon and Christian Moe, *Creating Historical Drama.*

24. Jessica Abbe, "Anne Bogart's Journeys," *TDR* 24:2 (1980), 85–100; Mariella Sandford, "Danny Mydlack: Suburban Cultural Worker," *TDR* 31:4 (1987),

91–108; Trudy Scott, "The Audience of One: Jamie Leo," *TDR* 23:1 (1979), 49–54.

25. Roger Scruton, *Art and Imagination: A Study in the Philosophy of Mind* (London, 1974), 170.

26. Bullough, "Psychical Distance," 92.

27. See the essays collected in Nikolai Evreinov, *The Theatre in Life,* trans. Alexander Nazaroff (New York, 1927).

PART THREE

Audience Improvisation

✳ ✳ ✳ ✳ ✳   Psychic Polyphony

UNTIL RELATIVELY MODERN TIMES, Western theatrical theory has been largely dominated by an orientation toward the dramatic script, and the techniques and procedures developed for the analysis of dramatic structures and phenomena were often essentially the same as those already successfully employed in the analysis of nondramatic literary texts. Unquestionably such strategies have provided a rich variety of insights, but at the same time, they have obscured important aspects of theatre, especially when these were not readily accessible to the sort of analysis developed for material created for reading rather than for enactment.

In recognition of this, much modern theatrical theory has followed the direction exemplified by Marco de Marinis, who has argued that the performed play cannot be built upon or projected from the "virtual mise en scene of the printed text, which has its own semiotic." Instead it must be viewed as a new phenomenon, a "spectacle text" which employs the written text only as one element in a multicoded, multidimensional, and pluralistic new textual system.[1]

Early in this century Stark Young suggested that the stage performance should be viewed as a "translation" of a text into another artistic "language,"[2] but this metaphor can be misleading unless one acknowledges that the process is not really akin to changing from one linguistic system to another but rather from one expressive system into another which is phenomenologically different. Many semioticians have suggested that the performed play "speaks" not one language but many, emitting what Barthes called "a thickness of signs."[3] Bert States, however, has called attention to an extremely important commonality among the various sign-systems employed by the theatre, suggesting that most of these produce "a language whose words consist to an unusual degree of things that *are* what they seem to be."[4]

Nothing is more basic to the theatrical experience than this physical reality. "A play," says Thornton Wilder, "visibly represents pure existing, while a novel is a past reported in the present, what one mind, claiming to omniscience, asserts to have existed."[5] The written text of the play occupies a somewhat uneasy position between these two. The omniscient narrator typical of the novel is not fully manifested here, but even so the drama does not reach us directly, but filtered through a quasi-authorial presence most obviously manifested in the stage directions. With an author like Shaw, the stage directions take us almost into the generic realm of the short story or novel, but even a dramatist as sparing in such indications as Shakespeare provides occasional suggestions for setting or movement, and of course must attribute all lines to the proper speaker. Clearly, reading the printed "Bernardo: Who's there?" is an experience much closer to reading the novelistic " 'Who's there?' cried Bernardo" than to seeing and hearing an actor speak this line. The roots of the words "theatre" (from *theatron,* a place for seeing), "spectator" (from *spectare,* to watch), and "auditorium" (from *audire,* to hear) all reflect the necessary physicality and presence of the theatre experience.

Theatrical performance thus occupies a strange, even uncanny position midway between arts of absence, such as the novel or the cinema, and the experience of presence we have in everyday life. Indeed, David Cole sees the essence of the theatre's power as resting precisely in this doubleness, where all elements—actors, scenery, lighting, etc.—exist both in themselves and as part of the mythical *illud tempus,* both as realities and as ideograms.[6]

This element of presence gives to all theatrical signs what States calls an affective corporeality, a certain irreducible "thingness," which may in fact interfere at times with their most efficient use as aesthetic devices. It was precisely this corporeality of theatrical signs which led Charles Lamb to consider all performances of Shakespeare inevitably inferior to reading. The reading of a tragedy he called "a fine abstraction. It presents to the fancy just so much of external appearances as to make us feel that we are among flesh and blood, while by far the greater and better part of our imagination is employed upon the thoughts and internal machinery of the character." In reading, "some dim images of royalty—a crown and sceptre, may float before our eyes" without durability or clear definition, while staging requires "full and cumbersome" coronation robes and the "shiftings and re-reshiftings of a Romish priest at mass."[7]

It is easy to see why Lamb prefers the flexibility and artistic control of "externals" offered by the written text. Here precisely as much detail and duration can be given to an object like a crown as the situation requires, from a fleeting image to a richly described artifact, and such an image can be instantly evoked or dismissed. The theatre, however, normally requires a real object with physical substance and permanence which demands the attention of both actors and audience. Unquestionably Lamb has isolated a critical difference between theatre and the written text, but while stressing the advantages gained by the written text through the absence of permanent corporeal objects, he has ignored the compensatory effects available to performance through an artistic utilization of such objects.

It is true that a physical crown provides no "dim image of royalty," but it may be a powerful visual metaphor, the strength of which has been recognized by dramatists in all ages. The triumphant rebel holding at last the physical symbol of power in his hands or the dying despot whose fallen crown has rolled just beyond the reach of his grasping fingers are the sort of powerful images that fix an entire dramatic situation in our imagination and our memory. Indeed, Goethe defines the theatrical in terms of just this sort of physical embodiment, "immediately symbolic to the eye," citing as an example the moment when Prince Hal removes the crown from his sleeping father, places it upon his own head, and struts proudly about.[8] Similarly the robing of the new pope in Brecht's *Galileo* takes advantage of precisely the ponderous presence which so troubled Lamb to create a powerful and memorable theatrical sequence.

Duration is often combined with presence to create striking effects on the stage completely unrealizable in print. Barthes in *Image, Music, Text* suggests that a text should no longer be regarded as a line of words releasing a single "theological" meaning (the "message of an author-God"), but as a multidimensional space "in which a variety of meanings, none of them original, blend and clash."[9] This spatial conception of a text as a field in which many voices compete for attention has a distinctly theatrical flavor, since the author-God is much more clearly a *Dieu caché* on the stage than in the written text. Certain voices are given corporeal reality, and the multidimensional space is not figurative but real. This Barthean view of a multivocal text has proven enormously fruitful in modern critical analysis, but the form of the written text will always guarantee that such multiplicity cannot be directly realized there, as it can in the theatre. Many voices may indeed be present in a written text, but all must be channeled by the nature of the medium into the single expressive device of the written line. Jindrîch Honzl spoke of words, actors, costumes, scenery, and music in the theatre as working in sharp contrast to this single "conductor," as being "different conductors of a single current that either passes from one to another or flows through several at one time."[10]

The single conductive line of the written text presents a serious obstacle to the author who wishes to keep an idea or an image steadily in the reader's mind while speaking of other things. In fact there is no literary device which can guarantee the permanence in the reader's consciousness of anything the words themselves are not at that moment considering. Lamb's "dim images" of crown and sceptre may well drift away as the text focuses on other matters even when the author *wants* them to remain present. The multiple channels of theatrical reception, however, allow simultaneous statements to be made by a variety of presences, often with powerful emotional effect. In Ingmar Bergman's *King Lear,* the crown, taken off by Lear in the first scene, remains downstage near the footlights throughout the play (even during the intermission, when it is picked out by a soft spotlight) as a constant and moving reminder of the initial disruptive act and of the subsequent leaderless condition of the realm.

Costumes and scenery almost inevitably make some kind of continuing commentary in the theatre. Thus an audience remains constantly aware, whatever else may be happening, of the steady rain and gloom outside the Alving house in *Ghosts,* of the formidable array of ancestral portraits surrounding poor Johannes Rosmer in *Romersholm,* of the heavy presence of the two great overarching elm trees in *Desire Under the Elms* which, if O'Neill's stage directions are followed, "brood oppressively over the house . . . like exhausted women resting their sagging breasts and hands and hair on its roof."[11] When these texts are merely read, it is most difficult, once the opening stage directions are passed, to keep such images visually present in the mind as other matters clamor for attention.

The multiple perception of presences is unquestionably a central feature in the particular power of the theatre. Mukařovský, summarizing the contributions of the Prague Linguistic Circle in his 1941 article "On the Current State of the Theory of the Theatre," observed that the theatre is essentially "an interplay of forces moving through time and space and pulling the spectator into the interplay which we call a stage production, a performance."[12] Only recently has theatre theory again begun to address this insight and to recognize that a production must in theory and in practice be conceived in time, must be considered from multiple and simultaneous perspectives, and must recognize all the while that every viewing will put together these perspectives in different combinations.

Even more central to the power of theatre than the various "presences" of properties, scenery, and other visual and auditory elements are the living presences of the actors, whose various psychic drives also "blend and clash" in a particularly striking and powerful manner. To this specifically theatrical phenomenon I have assigned the term "psychic polyphony." Some of the workings and implications of this phenomenon will be the central concern of the present essay.

In performance, characters, like crowns, utilize duration and presence to create a complex perceptual web which, thanks to the simultaneous accessibility of different "conductors" in performance, allows the spectator a freedom of response quite different from and more inclusive than that offered by the printed text. Modern reader-response theory has stressed the creative role of the reader in engaging a text, but whatever the freedom open to the interpretative process, the arrangement of stimuli upon which this interpretation is based is controlled to a far greater extent on the printed page. It is true that directors, designers, and actors do not *normally* encourage a free play of audience focus about the stage (although certain modern experimental performances have stood out as exceptions to the norm). An important part of theatre art traditionally has been that of guiding the spectators' attention to the proper element of the spectacle. Cultural norms also help to discourage a "free play" of attention across a perceptual field. Nevertheless, all theatre practitioners realize that focus on stage, as opposed to focus in print, is loosely controlled and that while the average audience may devote the major part of its attention to the central focus of the scene, this will almost invariably be supplemented with selective and personally chosen attention to secondary areas of focus, and even to characters and scenic elements not currently stressed at all. The very fact that the stage makes the elms or the portraits of Rosmer's ancestors accessible whether they are being spoken of or not means that the spectator may at any time give them primary focus, according to the free play of his or her desire or predisposition.

This relative freedom of the theatrical spectator to select the object of focus and to create an unique and individual synchronic "reading" as the play moves forward diachronically has particular implications for the way characters are created, sustained, and perceived on the stage. A long-standing rule for actors is to remember that no matter how small their part, whenever they are on stage someone is likely always to be giving them central, even if momentary, attention. The theatre has sought, with differing success in different periods, to accommodate this wandering focus by training its minor actors to present a clear contribution to the main action. The inanimate object on stage, so long as it can be initially assimilated into the world of the play, presents no further problem. But the actor, who shares the audience's double awareness of reality and pretence, must continually demonstrate to the spectator that he is "in character," since the fact that he is physically present serves always as a reminder of this "real" existence, an existence that may be foregrounded at any moment by choice, by inattention, or by some mishap.

The indifference of some producers to this matter aroused much protest in the nineteenth century while directors such as Saxe-Meiningen, Antoine, and Stanislavski were lauded for their efforts to ensure that every character on stage, no matter how insignificant, was at all times a fit subject for audience contemplation. In a memorable passage in Stanislavski's *Creating A Role*, the Stanislavski-like director Tortsov demonstrates something of the attention that went into such an effect by interrogating an extra who is playing a gondolier in *Othello*. Although this extra appears only as part of the crowd aroused by Iago and Roderigo at Brabantio's house at the opening of the play, Tortsov expects him to know his position in the household, his duties, his relation to his fellows and master, so that when he appears on stage it will be as a fully developed individual pursuing an action thought out and motivated in impressive detail.[13] A spectator focusing upon this gondolier should discover an element contributing distinctly to the total flow of the action just as Iago is.

Among the recent strategies for the analysis of the creation and interpretation of dramatic characters have been several showing a clear debt to the narratological structuralist analyses of Propp and Greimas. Although neither of these was primarily interested in the drama, their work has in turn reawakened interest in two hitherto rather neglected dramatic theorists with similar structural concerns, Georges Polti and Etienne Souriau, both of whom proposed dramatic taxonomies based upon "dramatic situations." For Polti these were a somewhat whimsical collection of nouns such as "madness," "adultery," and "disaster," and of phrases such as "all sacrificed for a passion," "falling prey to misfortune," or "necessity of sacrificing loved ones."[14] Souriau developed a more complex analysis based on six "functions"—the "thematic force" which seeks a goal, the goal sought, the receiver of profit from this goal, an opposing force, a helper, and an arbitrator.[15] Greimas' six actantial roles—subject, object, sender, receiver, opponent, and helper—are closely related to Souriau's functions and have been similarly employed for the analysis of dramatic structure.

Critics of this approach have complained of its taxonomic rigidity and its focus upon distribution of roles and relationships in an ultimately reductive manner. Actantial roles may shift rapidly about during a narrative, and a character may be simultaneously playing several roles in several different actions—subject in one; opponent, receiver, or helper in yet others. The physical plurality of theatrical performance makes this multiplicity particularly evident. Tortsov's conversation with the actor playing the gondolier reminds us that even the most minor character on the stage may be seen, and according to Stanislavski should be played, as the protagonist in his own life drama, responsible for the action, successful or not, which he attempts to carry out within the dramatic situation. In Stanislavskian terms he must seek the "creative objective at the heart of every motivational unit, an objective which carries in itself the germ of action."[16] The actions thus developed are united in what Stanislavski calls the through line of action leading toward the ultimate goal of the character, the superobjective.

Obviously, not all of the proposed actions of the various characters on stage can be fulfilled. As Stanislavski observes:

> No movement, striving, action is carried out on the stage, any more than in real life, without obstacles. One runs inevitably into the counter-movements and strivings of other people, or into conflicting events, or into obstacles caused by the elements, or other hindrances. Life is an unremitting *struggle*, one overcomes or one is defeated. Likewise on the stage, side-by-side with the through action there will be a series of counter-through actions on the part of other characters, other circumstances. The collision and conflict of these two opposing through actions constitute the dramatic situation.[17]

For our present purposes, the key concept in this description is "side-by-side," since it is precisely this that characterizes the theatrical, as opposed to the novelistic, presentation of an actantial web. No matter who is speaking or taking the center focus, we have the option as spectators to place our own focus on any other psychic presence on stage, and thus to interpret the pattern of actions and counter-actions in a great variety of ways at the same theatrical moment. Figure and ground here may be thought of as simultaneous to one another.

An important part of the unique power of the theatre has always derived from this psychic polyphony—the simultaneous expression of a number of different psychic lines of action, allowing the spectator a choice of focus and a variety in the process of combination. The potential power of mere physical and psychic presence, even (and sometimes especially) when a character speaks little or not at all, was clearly recognized from the beginning of Western drama. The silence of Cassandra for almost three hundred lines after her entrance with Agamemnon in the *Oresteia* is a device of enormous power on stage, though in the printed text her presence during the emotion-packed scene between Agamemnon and Clythemnestra may be almost totally forgotten. In the theatre, however, like the crown in Bergman's *Lear*, simply by her presence she brings to our mind, as Kitto observes, "a whole train of associated ideas, like a remembered scent or tune."[18] At the same time, through our continual realization of the steadily growing emotional investment she has in the scene being enacted, she builds up during this extended period an overwhelming psychic expectation, discharged at last in her unearthly cry to Apollo, one of the most chilling moments in the Greek theatre.

In more normal stage interaction we see a constantly shifting pattern of actions and reactions, contributed to by everyone present and offering a multiple psychic perspective to the observer. The plays of Chekhov, with which, of course, Stanislavski is particularly associated, provide especially clear examples of psychic polyphony, and it is this, I would suggest, which makes Chekhov notoriously less effective in print than on the stage. It is extremely difficult, if not impossible, to read a play like *Three Sisters* or *The Cherry Orchard* while keeping a continuously clear idea of the physical presence and psychic plenitude of all of the characters on stage, especially of those with very little to say. It is harder still to focus freely among them to observe their reactions, gestures, and expressions no matter who is speaking, as one may so easily do in the theatre. Yet it is precisely this continuous interplay which lies at the very heart of the Chekhovian theatre.

Certain theatrical scenes seem created almost as if to call attention to this multiple perspective and certainly to capitalize upon it. One of the most famous is the play within a play in *Hamlet*. Here we have the players themselves as one (already multiple) focus of attention. We have the grouping Claudius, Gertrude, and Polonius, each watching the play, as we know, with quite different concerns. We have another grouping elsewhere on stage of Ophelia and Hamlet, watching the play, the king, and each other, and finally we have Horatio, stationed by Hamlet in yet another location to provide another perspective on the king's reactions. Horatio, of course, has also his own concerns, and we can be fairly certain that he will also be keeping a watchful eye on his beloved, if somewhat erratic, friend. To be complete, we should also include other members of the court—guards, ladies and gentlemen, and so on, whose reactions also distinctly contribute to the overall effect of the scene as presented, though they may well be forgotten when it is only read. The spectator has phenomenological access at every instant to every one of these perspectives.

An interesting contrast may be seen by comparing this scene as staged with any of its many filmed versions. The film, despite its heavy reliance upon visual and iconic representation, is, in respect to psychic polyphony, much closer to the written text than to the stage performance. This difference was recognized at least as early as Béla Balázs' pioneering study in film theory, which suggested that film became an independent art by creating its own "form-language." This was achieved by discarding the three "basic formal principles" of theatrical art, which, according to Balázs, were:

1. that the spectator sees the enacted scene as a whole in space, always seeing the whole of the space,

2. that the spectator always sees the stage from a fixed, unchanging distance, and

3. that the spectator's angle of vision does not change.

In the film, says Balázs, these principles are replaced by four "new Methods": varying distance between spectator and scene (and hence varying dimensions of scenes); division of the integral picture of the scene into sections of "shots"; changing angles, perspectives, and focus of these "shots"; and the assembling of the "shots" in montage.[19]

Most of these "new methods" involved the control of focus and perception, and moved the film from the more open perceptual world of the theatre to a more closely confined sequence like that of the novel. The spectators at Bergman's *Lear* may look at the crown at any time, but the cutting and montage of the film will govern precisely when that image is visually accessible, much as the novel governs when it is narratively accessible.

While the cinema was developing its own "language," these devices of selection and focus seem to have encountered some resistance from spectators accustomed to the more total picture provided by the stage. Pioneer Robert Peguy told of an early producer who complained that visual focus excluding the legs and feet of actors might lead the audience to think that he was employing cripples, and D. W. Griffith is reported to have encountered similar literalistic resistance to the first close-ups, with giant, disembodied heads filling the entire screen.[20] Such stories have a somewhat apocryphal feeling, but whatever problems of interpretation the new filmic codes may originally have presented, they have now become culturally accepted, so that film is not only created, but also perceived in a quite different way from the theatre. Patrice Pavis has rightly observed that "even if there is no editing after the shooting of the film and if the scenes are shot from one fixed point with no camera change or close-ups, the video film imposes by its own particular framing a limited and *partial* vision. It is not useful for the camera to film the whole stage area even from an unchanging distance."[21] My own single experience with a full-length film, shot as a production record of a performance in Salzburg from a single fixed position in the audience and with the entire stage always visible, absolutely supported this observation. The performance seemed astonishingly flat, lifeless, and remote, quite unlike the usual experience of either film or theatre.

The theatrical tableau has often been used as a striking device for calling attention to psychic polyphony by holding it, as it were, on a sustained chord. A well-known example is the screen scene in Sheridan's *The School for Scandal*. Robert Scholes has called the moment of revelation in this scene "one of the great moments of pure stagecraft in the history of the theatre," at which "all the layers of ironic perception are allowed to discharge into laughter and applause." The silent exchange of looks in the tableau, Scholes continues, "can be sustained as long as the actors can mime and the audience interpret additional nuances of meaning."[22]

The ironies of this classic scene and the audience's enjoyment of them depend precisely upon the psychic plurality which is a distinctive feature of theatre art. Each of the participants in this tableau—Joseph and Charles Surface, Lady Teazle and Sir Peter—brings to the scene his or her own fully developed character and line of action, and in this moment of comic crisis the audience's perception is free to wander freely, relishing the variety of reactions and interrelations simultaneously available. Wherever one looks there is a new source of delight, and each spectator may choose the order in which he or she reads the scene—focusing upon Joseph's discomforture, Charles' delight, Lady Teazle's embarrassment, or Sir Peter's astonishment—in whatever order or whatever combination proves most attractive. This freedom might be contrasted with a filming of the same scene, where the camera would inevitably make these choices for us, devoting a set number of frames in a set order to close-ups of each of the participants for a totally different phenomenological effect.

Many memorable moments in the theatre are built upon this same device. The discovery of Natasha and Belyev by Rakitin and Arkady in the fourth act of Turgenev's *A Month in the Country* has a dynamic closely analogous to Sheridan's scene and generates a similar prolonged delight in the audience. In each of these examples the psychic interchange continues during the period of physical paralysis, since the characters are reacting not only to the new situation but also to each other's reactions.

A somewhat different effect is obtained when everyone on stage reacts simultaneously to a single stimulus, but without particular attention to one another. A notable example of such a tableau concludes Gogol's *Inspector General,* and the author describes it in careful detail:

> The Mayor stands in the centre, looking like a post, with outspread arms and head thrown back. To his right are his Wife and Daughter, each straining towards him with all her body. Behind them is the Postmaster, who has turned into a living question mark addressed to the spectators. Behind him is the Superintendent of Schools, most guilelessly nonplussed. Behind him, near the very side of the proscenium, are three Lady Guests, leaning together with the most sarcastic expressions on their faces, meant for the Mayor and still more for this Wife and Daughter. To the left of the Mayor is the Director of Charities, with his head somewhat cocked, as though he were listening to something. Behind him is the Judge, with his arms spread wide, squatting almost to the ground, and with his lips puckered as if to whistle, or to say, "Oh, my sainted aunt! This is it, sure enough!" Behind him is Korobkin, turning to the spectators with one eye narrowed and putting over a caustic insinuation concerning the Mayor. Behind him, at the very side of the pros-

cenium, are Dobchinski and Bobchinski, the arrested motion of their hands directed at each other, their mouths gaping and their eyes goggling at each other. The other Guests remain where they are, like so many pillars of salt. All the characters, thus petrified, retain their positions for almost a minute and a half.

(Slow Curtain[23])

The Gogol tableau stands somewhere between the tableau emphasizing a moment of intense psychic interplay, like those in *The School for Scandal* and *A Month in the Country,* and another sort of tableau where the primary interest is not psychic, but pictorial or emblematic. The psychic tableau attempts to justify itself to some extent realistically—its participants remain frozen in shock or surprise as they might in a similar crisis in real life. Emblematic tableaux are not, of course, devoid of psychological content, but the justification for the "freezing" of the scene is usually not psychological, but pictorial, as in the nineteenth-century melodramas where all the actors at a moment of high excitement struck simultaneously "attitudes" to form an applause-attracting "picture," or when stage action is developed so as to lead to a visual "quotation" of a famous painting or sculptural group, and the action freezes not for internal reasons, but simply so that the reproduction can be appreciated. Cross-fertilization of narrative paintings and theatre was particularly popular during the nineteenth century, when certain plays were created primarily to provide scenes reproducing famous paintings and when painters often selected as subjects scenes in plays (Shakespeare being particularly favored).[24]

The simultaneous access to elements in the narrative painting seems to provide an opportunity of "reading" similar to that offered by the theatre, but the fact that the theatrical scene is composed of actually existing elements embedded in time creates in truth a quite different totality of impression. In a narrative painting we can consider either pictorial or emotive qualities (at least those that can be deduced from a frozen moment) at our leisure, knowing that every element of the composition "will stay 'til we come."

We can also let our attention play over an emblematic tableau in the theatre without pressure of time, but only so long as we regard it pictorially, seeing the persons in it as inanimate parts of a visual composition. As soon as we allow ourselves to remember, as we invariably must, that they are also living beings, we must take into consideration both their psychic and physical reality, thus exposing the artificiality and arbitrariness of the tableau itself. Their immobility then takes on other meanings and raises other questions. It becomes problematic, and we therefore begin to speculate about its purpose. Is the character stunned, frightened, confused? Or (in a more presentational style of performance) has the actor consciously offered a pose for our contemplation and is continuing to hold it by an act of will? In any case, in the living world of the theatre, such stasis soon registers as alien, and its prolongation arouses an inevitable tension, either pleasurable or disturbing. We may share the delight of Sir David Wilkie, who called a staged *tableau vivant* "the most beautiful reality I ever saw," but we share also his recognition of the inevitable effect of entropy on this artificially maintained beauty: "so evanescent is the group, that the curtain drops in twenty seconds, the people being unable to remain for any longer period in one precise position."[25] A delightful theatrical illustration of this recognition is offered by *The Fantasticks*, which closes its first act on the sort of highly artificial posed tableau beloved by nineteenth-century producers (this tableau is often used as a visual emblem for the New York production). The second act opens with the same tableau, but it gradually dissolves and collapses as fatigue and the pressures of changing psychic interests affect its various members. The outstanding recent example of the common nineteenth-century practice of developing an entire play around the stage re-creation of a well-known portrait is surely Sondheim's *Sunday in the Park with George*, the first act of which concludes with the stage re-creation of Seurat's *A Sunday Afternoon on the Island of La Grande Jatte*. The second act, like that of *The Fantasticks*, begins with the same tableau, but now that it is continued, our reaction shifts from the visual delight of the re-creation to the tension engendered by the enforced immobility of what we now focus on as living presences. The opening song of this act, "It's Hot up Here," sung as the tableau is maintained, expresses the continuing discomfort of those beings trapped in Seurat's "painting." Even frozen in position, however, their psychic interplay continues ("The soldiers have forgotten us"). Gogol's guests may stand "like pillars of salt," but our knowledge that they are not pillars of salt creates a tension which in this case (through the conflict between the living and mechanical discussed by Bergson) is released in laughter. A painting of the same scene might arouse amusement through the guests' expressions or physical appearance, but hardly through their immobility.

The mutability of dramatic sign may, as Bogatyrev and Honzl have observed, result in an actor's being treated according to a particular theatrical convention as an abstract quality or even an inanimate object,[26] but it is almost impossible to prevent the psychic presence of the actor from "bleeding through" the convention and thus continuing to affect the reception of the piece. *Sunday in the Park with George* plays amusingly upon the difference between the live actor who becomes an element in a tableau and the tableau representation of an actor without life in the two soldiers from the painting. The productions of Taduesz Kantor have constructed tableaux of mixed living figures and dummies for a much more chilling and grotesque response to this disjuncture. Shakespeare explores the comic potential of life "bleeding through" in his depiction of the laborers of Athens appearing as "Wall" and "Moonshine" in the interlude of Pyramus and Thisbe in *A Midsummer Night's Dream.*

The insistence of psychic presence adds piquancy to the emblematic tableau on stage, but it also adds a certain instability which is not always in the best interests of the desired frozen "effect." The statue of the Commandatore in *Don Giovanni,* for example, is always a bit distracting, since the audience generally (correctly) assumes that the statue is being counterfeited by a real actor and is thus highly sensitive not only to any inadvertent movement before the statue "comes to life," but also to the psychic presence emanating even from a very rigid figure which they seek to "read into" the psychic polyphony of the scene.

Even dramatists sometimes seem to feel that their lesser characters function like lesser characters in a novel, existing only to the degree that they are created by the author and thus condemned, like Lamb's images of royalty, to only that portion of existence required by the machinery of the action. Thus Strindberg in his preface to *Miss Julie* says that he deliberately portrayed the supporting character of Christine in a "somewhat abstract" manner because "ordinary people are, to a certain degree, abstract in the performance of their daily work—conventional, and showing only one side of themselves—and as long as the spectator feels no need to see their other sides, my abstract portrayal of them will serve well enough."[27] It is true that we learn less about the character Christine during this play than about Jean or Miss Julie, but when portrayed by a real, living actress, she is in no way more abstract than they, and while she is on stage makes just as legitimate a claim to audience attention.

Dramatically speaking, a character may be "unrealized," as the Son claims to be in Pirandello's *Six Characters in Search of an Author,* but he can no more project a "dim image" of a person than the stage crown can present Lamb's "dim image of royalty." When such a character appears on the stage, the physical and psychic presence of the actor who embodies him will necessarily provide an unavoidable measure of realization. A character on stage may be unclear or inconsistent, but he will always necessarily participate fully in the diverse structure of presence, and thus in the changeable tensions of the drama's reception. Whether an actor has developed a particular contextual world, like Stanislavski's gondolier, or not, as a living being he possesses always the potential of being viewed as the protagonist of his own drama, entangled with and yet separate from the drama of every other character. Thus the web of competing through-lines of action, which Stanislavski considered the basis of the dramatic situation, is always potentially involved in the theatre. Analysis like his encourages us to recognize at least some of the ways in which the multiplicity of actantial patterns, which I have called psychic polyphony, make a central contribution to the almost endless variety of readings constantly offered by theatrical performance, and beyond that, to the specifically theatrical pleasure offered by this freedom of reading and the simultaneity of multiple perception.

NOTES

1. Marco de Marinis, "Lo spettacolo come testo 1," *Versus* 21 (Sept.–Dec. 1978), 57. All translations, unless otherwise noted, are my own.
2. Stark Young, "Translations," *Immortal Shadows* (New York: C. Scribner's Sons, n.d.), 3.
3. Roland Barthes, *Critical Essays*, trans. Richard Howard (Evanston, 1972), 262. Tadeusz Kowzan analyzes thirteen different theatrical sign systems in "The Sign in the Theatre," *Diogenes* 61 (1968), 52–80.
4. Bert O. States, *Great Reckonings in Little Rooms* (Berkeley, 1985), 20.
5. Thornton Wilder, "Some Thoughts on Playwriting," *The Intent of the Artist*, ed. Augusto Centeno (Princeton, 1941), 89.
6. David Cole, *The Theatrical Event: A "Mythos," A Vocabulary, a Perspective* (Middletown, Conn., 1975), 155–56.
7. Charles Lamb, "On the Tragedies of Shakespeare, Considered with Reference to Their Fitness for Stage Representation," *The Works of Charles and Mary Lamb*, ed. E. V. Lucas, 5 vols. (New York, 1903), 1:110–11.
8. Johann Wolfgang von Goethe, *Sämtliche Werke*, 40 vols. (Stuttgart, 1902–07) 26:52.
9. Roland Barthes, *Image, Music, Text*, trans. Stephen Heath (New York, 1977), 146.
10. Jindřich Honzl, "Dynamics of the Sign in the Theatre," trans. Irwin Titunik, *Semiotics of Art: Prague School Contributions*, ed. Ladislau Matejka and Irwin Titunik (Cambridge, Mass., 1976), 91.
11. Eugene O'Neill, *The Plays of Eugene O'Neill*, 3 vols. (New York, 1941), 1:202.
12. Jan Mukařovský, "On the Current State of the Theory of the Theatre," *Structure, Sign, and Function*, trans. John Burbank and Peter Steiner (New Haven, 1978), 203.
13. Constantin Stanislavski, *Creating a Role*, trans. E. R. Hapgood (New York, 1961), 8.
14. Georges Polti, "Les 36 situations dramatiques," *Mercure de France* 12 (1894).
15. Etienne Souriau, *Les deux cent mille situations dramatiques* (Paris, 1950), 144.
16. Stanislavski, *An Actor Prepares*, trans. E. R. Hapgood (New York, 1936), 110.
17. Stanislavski, *Creating a Role*, 80.
18. H. D. F. Kitto, *Greek Tragedy* (London, 1950), 76.
19. Béla Balázs, *Theory of the Film*, trans. Edith Bone (New York, 1953), 30–31.
20. Maurice Bardech, *The History of Motion Pictures*, trans. Iris Barry (New York, 1938), 13.
21. Patrice Pavis, *Languages of the Stage*, trans. Susan Melrose (New York, 1982), 123.
22. Robert Scholes, *Semiotics and Interpretation* (New Haven, 1982), 79.
23. Nikolay Gogol, *Taras Bulba; The Inspector General*, trans. B. G. Guerney (London, 1962) 409–10.

24. This interplay, with related phenomena in literature, has been studied in Martin Meisel, *Realizations* (Princeton, 1983).

25. Allan Cunningham, *The Life of Sir David Wilkie*, 3 vols. (London, 1843) 2:333.

26. Peter Bogatyrev, "Forms and Functions of Folk Theatre," trans. Bruce Kochis, and Honzl, "Dynamics of the Sign," *Semiotics of Art*, ed. Matejka and Titunik 51–56; 74–93.

27. August Strindberg, *Plays*, trans. Michael Meyer (New York, 1964), 107.

✳ ✳ ✳ ✳ ✳   Local Semiosis and
                Theatrical Interpretation

IN HIS ESSAY "Art as a Cultural System," Clifford Geertz argues that the central connection between art and collective life should be sought not, as it has been through much of Western aesthetic theory, on an instrumental or functional level, but at a semiotic one. Works of art do not, he feels, celebrate social structures or forward useful doctrines except in quite indirect ways. What they do is materialize a way of experiencing. They "bring a particular cast of mind out into the world of objects, where men can look at it."[1]

So semiotic a concern seems highly contemporary, but Shakespeare gives a strikingly similar observation to the Athenian Duke Theseus in the final act of *A Midsummer Night's Dream*, within the famous passage concerning the lunatic, the lover, and the poet: "as imagination bodies forth/The forms of thing unknown, the poet's pen/Turns them to shapes, and gives to airy nothing/A local habitation and a name."

Of course, the habitation must be local. However general may be the "airy nothing" with which the poet begins, when it is brought into the world of objects, given a name and a situation, then that process must inevitably be conditioned by the artistic tools of the artist's own culture and by the ways that culture defines and interprets artistic artifacts. Thus the work of art may be considered a manifestation of cultural experience, a way of being in the world.

Such a view of the work of art is surely a useful corrective to the naive assumption that such a work makes once and for all a specific "aesthetic" statement, the same for all audiences, whatever their cultural background, and it is not difficult to see why an anthropologically oriented theorist in particular should find congenial an approach to art which would privilege the unique cultural context of the work over its possible universality. In support of this orientation, Geertz summarizes some of the arguments of art historian Michael Baxandall concerning fifteenth-century Italian painting.

Whatever the painter's own special professional skills, Baxandall observes, "he is himself a member of the society he works for and shares its visual experience and habit."[2] The artist and his public in any culture and at any period share particular local conventions and codes for the creation and experiencing of works of art which are not solely "artistic" conventions, but all manner of life-structuring assumptions operative in that culture. Since we are no longer participants in that culture, we can of course no longer assume that we see the painting in terms of the same codes or conventions which were operative at its creation. Hence, Baxandall observes, an old picture must be considered as a record of visual activity that one has to learn to read, just as one has to learn to read a text from a different culture, a strategy which Geertz approvingly quotes.

The powerful influence of new criticism in literary studies earlier in this century and parallel critical assumptions about self-contained or self-sufficient works in painting or other arts have provided a cultural background against which Baxandall's point may seem more original than it really is. Romantic theorists routinely insisted upon the necessity of understanding works in historical context; Taine and the positivists called for the analysis of artistic creativity in these terms; Wilhelm Dilthey and most of the generation of German scholars who followed him approached the work of art as an objective symbol of the artist's psychic reaction to his particular cultural situation, the *Weltanschauung*. In more recent times, one hardly has to read far in semiotic theory to come across the idea that interpretive codes are culturally determined, and that an understanding of how a quattrocento painting came to be created as it was in the first place and of the reactions it sought to gain or did gain from contemporary viewers would require an understanding of the cultural codes operative at that particular historical period.

Without denying the importance of this concern, or the worthiness of the kind of historical study Geertz and Baxandall advocate, we must bear in mind a number of important limitations of such an approach. The first is one basic to all questions of historical hermeneutics and indeed is a basic theme of much of Geertz' writings—and that is the enormous difficulty of determining, from outside any culture, what codes are operating in the culture, as well as their relative importance and their interrelationships. The difficulty need not discourage attempts, but it should encourage humility and a recognition that learning to "read" an old picture in the way it was originally "meant to be read" may be closer to a pious hope than a particular critical choice.

The movement of works of art through time adds to the complexity of this hermeneutic problem. Like any cultural artifact removed either temporally or spatially from an originating context, the work of art becomes then open to new interpretations, the result, we might say, of entering a new local semiosis. There are several reasons why works of art create particularly complex examples of this process. First, since the designation of an object as an artwork accords it a culturally privileged position, special care is often taken for its preservation, a care which makes such artifacts more likely than many others to survive their original cultural context and begin to move through other cultures, thus becoming open to changing interpretive strategies. Moreover, the work of art, being generally considered a highly charged semiotic object, for this reason tends to generate a "tradition" of critical commentary and interpretation as it moves through time. Few persons would challenge the validity of seeking the "meaning" of a quattrocento painting, or of finding this meaning to be rich and complex, but probably only anthropologists, semioticians, and similar specialized speculators upon cultural phenomena would be as likely to seek the "meaning" of a quattrocento utensil for eating or grooming.

Thus as the work of art moves through time and through different cultural surroundings, it accumulates interpretations, and these not infrequently become associated with the work, affecting subsequent interpretation perhaps as much as the work itself. An excellent example can be seen in perhaps the world's best-known painting, the Mona Lisa of Leonardo da Vinci. The Oxford *History of World Art* begins its discussion of this work with what seems a comment about the originating conditions, indeed the only such comment in the passage devoted to it. "She had been saddened by the loss of children, and it is said that Leonardo employed musicians to charm a wan smile to her reluctant lips."[3] By whom, we might ask, is this said? Not, in fact, by contemporaries of the painter, but by historians of the romantic period who found in this painting that tension between opposing emotions which was so important to romantic consciousness. Thanks to them the famous "wan smile," never observed in the previous centuries of the painting's existence, became a part of its cultural codification and a phenomenon to be "explained" historically. The much-publicized recent theory of the painting's origin, calling it a hidden self-portrait of the artist, does not neglect to mention that this centuries-old secret joke helps to explain the famous enigmatic smile.

Thus a work of art from another local semiosis is both more and less than what it was within that semiotic environment—less, because of what we have irretrievably lost, and more, because the work comes to us with semiotic additions from intervening contexts. Nor should we view these accumulations as negative "encrustations" which must be cleared away to see the work as it "really is." It is only through their mediation that the work has come down to us at all, and it may be, as Gadamer, for example, argues, that we are able to make a viable interpretive connection with the original work only because of the mediating and connecting tradition, of which that work itself has become a part. Our own encounter with the work, of course, is different yet from the summing up of the tradition, although that tradition almost invariably conditions the encounter. We come to the work not only with the expectations engendered by its own tradition and the traditions of similar objects, but with all of the rest of the cultural expectations of our own society, just as each new audience for the work has done through time.

The particular artistic phenomenon which I propose to consider today, the theatre, requires us to engage these concerns in a more direct and radical way than do most of the other arts, since the theatre displays in a particularly striking way the effects of changes in local semiosis. A quattrocento painting may undergo enormous changes in visual reading as it is experienced in times and places far from its origin, but it remains the same object, a fact which sometimes obscures the importance of the changes in strategies for understanding it. Theatre, however, as a *performed* art, creates no total artifact available for subsequent experience and interpretation. Every performance is unique and unrepeatable, understood by whatever codes are available to that audience at that specific cultural moment.

This ability—indeed, necessity—for theatre to continue an active engagement with changing cultural codes (as distinct from the passive engagement of painting) makes it a particularly interesting and complex participant among the arts in local semiosis. Dance and music, the other major temporal arts, share something of this uniqueness of occasion, but neither in quite the same way as theatre, at least within the Western tradition. When specific dance works are revived, often by the same company, the normal practice is to attempt something physically very close to the original. Musical compositions are far less closely tied to any specific performance than dance compositions, and a moderately trained ear can easily detect differences in the interpretations of several orchestras playing the same score. The differences are far more extreme, however, if one looks instead to a variety of stagings of the same dramatic script—for example, a play by Shakespeare.

If we try to apply Baxandall's strategy to the theatre and seek to learn how to "read" a play in its original *performance* terms, we encounter all sorts of difficulties. Using a painting as an intellectual model distorts our thinking about this process considerably, because it encourages us to posit a public encounter with a specific artistic object in an equally specific historical context. Since a performance is not an object with a certain permanence, like a painting, but an unreproducible event, even to speak of the "original" performance raises historical questions of great complexity. What *is* the original performance? The first given before an audience? If so, then what is an audience? What if the play is first read? What if, like the plays of Büchner, it is never performed at all until many years after the death of its creator and in a very different cultural context than that of its written composition? Or what if it is first given a "private" showing to a small public? If such showings count, how small can the public be? Or how public? What if only one or two critics, or one censor, or a bored monarch is present? Does a reading by the author to the future actors qualify as a first performance? Or a reading by the actors without staging? On the other hand, what if a play has a conventional "opening night" and subsequently is radically altered? Or what if a play goes through a number of revisions, all publicly presented?

The standard response to these questions has generally been to ignore them and to take refuge in a comfortable illusion, which is that the performed play is essentially preserved in the written text, a historical artifact which may stand in for the absent performance and be regarded as the theatrical equivalent of the quattrocento painting. It is easy to see the appeal of this illusion. The script is a tangible object which, like the painting, may exist over a considerable period of time. Also like the painting, of course, it may be reinterpreted or even in historical terms misinterpreted by later readers applying altered interpretive codes, but the play itself remains the object it is, presumably, still accessible to its original codes if a historical critic, following Baxandall's advice, can discover and apply them.

The existence of this object encourages the view that behind the printed text lies a specific performance, which may be taken as the performance "original," although the texts which remain from classic periods, from the Renaissance, and even in many cases from more recent times in fact may differ widely from the words actually spoken when the play represented by those texts was first realized in the theatre. In many cases the surviving texts have been seriously corrupted or represent a "literary" reworking of theatrical material, but even when they can be taken as reasonably accurate transcripts of performance, they can hardly be expected to reproduce the inevitable minor variations of the living performance.

During many periods of theatre history, this fluidity of text has been frankly accepted by audience and actors alike, and even when it has been resisted in certain cultural situations, the resistance has had only minor or temporary effect. The Greek officials of the fourth century B.C. kept copies of the classic texts and instituted fines for actors who altered lines; Hamlet, doubtless reflecting the impatience of his creator, begged the obstreperous clowns to speak "no more than was set down for them"; Victor Hugo quarreled constantly with the actors of the Comedie Francaise about their reworking of his lines; nineteenth-century police inspectors frequently visited the theatres of Austria, Germany, Italy, and France to prevent actors from delivering material not approved by the censor; and Samuel Beckett and Arthur Miller have recently taken legal action against companies for departing from their texts, but all such efforts at controlling the libidinal flow of performance have failed, leaving intact a more basic tradition according to which dramatic scripts have always been cut, elaborated, or modified according to the exigencies of the performance situation. Persons unacquainted with this tradition often naively assume that the text of *King Lear* which they purchase in some bookstore represents the precise words spoken in performances of that play ever since Shakespeare's time. Those, however, with some knowledge of the history of Shakespearian performance will know that for most of the play's history it was radically altered in general plot, in specific details, and in wording, and that a concern for the establishment of a text close to Shakespeare's own has been a rather recent phenomenon. Indeed, this concern has still not resulted in the production of a text upon which all scholars can agree, and almost any modern performance, while it will normally not add material, will almost certainly make extensive cuts in whatever scholarly version serves as its starting point. Even the most formal literary modes do not necessarily hamper this process. Schiller was proud of the ability of the Weimar actors to extemporize in blank verse to cover forgotten lines or other problems, and classically trained French actors of the seventeenth and eighteenth centuries developed a similar facility even in Alexandrines.

A recognition of this fluidity reveals that even on the level of the written text, seemingly the most invariable part of the performance, theatre is extremely open to the operations of local semiosis. It is not really correct to regard the text, as Ingarden suggested, as a kind of unvarying "deep structure" for the enunciations of the individual performances, unless, perhaps, one looks deeper still, beyond the specific words to whatever pattern of action, arrangement of relationships, or cluster of motifs it is which allows us to cluster together all reworkings of, for example, the Faust story, whatever their individual manifestations.

The myth of origination, as Derrida has frequently pointed out, is a very powerful one, and perhaps nowhere more evident or more misleading than in this matter of the relationship between the written and the performed text. There have been major theorists ever since the romantic period who have recognized the tendency of performance to mediate material—that is, to respond to the changing expressive and interpretive codes of changing times—but most have complained of this tendency and opposed to it a "faithfulness" to the "original" written text, presumably unaffected by such changes and thus an unmediated expression of the original author's thought. Charles Lamb's famous essay "On the Tragedies of Shakespeare considered with reference to their fitness for stage representation" expresses precisely this fear of the mediation of performance, and advises the individual reading of the plays in the study as the surest way to experience clearly what Shakespeare had in mind.[4] Goethe took a somewhat more moderate view, suggesting that the plays could profitably be read aloud by a trained actor who could respond to them intelligently, but he still urged that they be read in as "neutral" a manner as possible.[5]

Even today, one encounters those who urge that the theatre produce plays by Shakespeare "straight," or "as the author intended," or to "let the plays speak for themselves," as if unmediated performance were desirable or even possible. Peter Brook has responded to this common advice as succinctly as anyone. "A play cannot speak for itself," he says; one must "conjure its sound from it."[6] Similarly Tyrone Guthrie has warned that the attempt to avoid interpretation usually results in the imitation of previous interpretations which have grown comfortably familiar.[7] It is important to remember that the performed play, unlike the painting, comes to us not as a specific object, but only through a performance tradition. It is rather as if we did not have da Vinci's Mona Lisa but only a large number of copies made during the past generation, themselves copied from copies of the previous generation, all the way back to the original painting, with the added difficulty that all intervening copies have disappeared along with the original. The most recent copies would probably have a quite unmistakable smile, but in the absence of external documentation we would have no way of knowing if the original had it. Thus when commentators speak of doing Shakespeare "correctly," they are much more likely to be thinking of a performance tradition, and probably a rather recent one, than of the essentially unrecoverable original conditions of performance. For generations actors playing Hamlet knocked over a chair in the queen's bedroom when the ghost appeared, assuming that the practice went back to Shakespeare. Indeed it may have, though we have no record of it before Betterton in the late seventeenth century, and it is unlikely that we will ever know for sure. Faced with the complexity not only of contemporary interpretation, but also with the accretions of an interpretive tradition, all more accessible than whatever first appeared on the stage, it is little wonder than some romantic theorists dreamed of somehow separating performance from interpretation.

Unhappily, an unmediated performance is a contradiction in terms. Even were the printed play the kind of invariable object that some theorists have incorrectly considered it to be, that object is not accessible to audiences except on those rare occasions when they bring texts to the theatre or purchase them in the lobby to read during the performance. On this matter Lamb was correct. A written text becomes quite another thing when it is enacted. The speaking of a text invariably interprets it, and no dramatist has yet devised (and few, indeed, have shown any interest in devising) a text which would absolutely control every nuance of its own physical delivery. On the contrary, Western dramatists have traditionally seemed willing to recognize that one of the conditions and fascinations of dramatic writing is the creation of texts open to changing interpretations.

Just how this openness is achieved has been the subject of a wide range of theoretical opinions. Anne Ubersfeld's characterization of the dramatic text as *troué*—possessing "holes" left open to the performance and, through that, to the concerns of a changed local semiosis—is a useful metaphor.[8] One must not, however, take it too literally and think of the text as composed of a specific solid and permanent part which allows from time to time specific spaces for improvisation, like the measures for improvisational solos in certain musical compositions. In fact every element of the dramatic text must be filtered through the interpretative process in performance, and thus there is no specific part which we can designate as text or as *trou*.

Another theoretical approach to the openness of the dramatic text to performance interpretation has been to compare it to translation. This was the approach of Croce and, after him, of Pirandello, and for both of them, as for Lamb, the translation was inevitably a diminishing process. Croce compared a performance of a Shakespearian play to a painting or a musical composition inspired by the play, at best a kind of simplified version for those unable to understand the original. Similarly Pirandello spoke of "scenic translations—so many actors, so many translations, more or less faithful, more or less fortunate, but like any translation, *always and necessarily* inferior to the original."[9] Here again we see the workings of the privileging of origination, and the assumption is the same as we have already seen in Lamb—that there exists a single, apprehensible original text, accessible to any intelligent reader, and offering an essentially invariable reading richer, more profound, and more correct than anything filtered through any interpretive process.

Aside from the highly questionable merits of this position intellectually, it frequently prevents us, as it prevented Croce and Lamb, from recognizing what positive value might be involved in the dynamic of an art form particularly open to changing interpretive codes. Yet the translation metaphor, despite certain disadvantages, can aid in the illustration of this process. It is important that we do not, like Pirandello and Croce, unquestioningly accept the dictum that all translation is always and necessarily inferior to the original, that no translation can compare with

Shakespeare in English, Molière in French, or Ibsen in Norwegian. Those actively involved in the production of an international repertoire realize that performance adds a new dimension to this question. Antony Sher, in his fascinating recent book *Year of the King,* describes the process of the creation of the character of Shakespeare's Richard III at a time while he was still performing Molière's Tartuffe, and he speaks often of the difficulty of finding a fresh and new approach to the ancient and overly familiar lines of Shakespeare, a problem far less acute for non-English actors playing the text, while no such problem existed for his own playing of Tartuffe in translation.[10] Translation does more than simply re-energize a passage so familiar that it is difficult both to deliver and to receive (such as "to be or not to be"). It also opens the written text much more readily to changing cultural codes. If we find the William Archer translations of Ibsen from the 1890s too stiff and Victorian, as most modern readers and playgoers do, we have been provided with excellent new translations approximately every ten to fifteen years since that time. Most of them leave the external Victorian world of the play intact, but make subtle adjustments to the speeches to fit our own changing speech patterns so that the dialogue continues to seem natural and unforced. The advantage that Norwegian audiences enjoy—direct access to Ibsen's original words—means at the same time that the written text cannot adjust so readily to changing cultural contexts, and a dramatist whose power in part derived from his sensitivity to everyday speech paradoxically often retains that power better in translation than in the original.

We touch here upon a specific instance of a much more general phenomenon which has extremely important implications not only for the theatrical performance, but also for semiotic theory in general. We have been speaking of local semiosis as a phenomenon not only of different systems of meaning in cultures in different geographical areas, but also of semiotic changes which occur through time (as in the reading of the quattrocento painting). The signifiers of that painting no longer for us refer to the same signified because of cultural changes in codes. It is at least theoretically possible, Geertz and Baxandall suggest, to overcome the barriers between our local semiotic systems and those in operation when the painting was created by learning the alien systems.

But Geertz admits that this goal probably cannot ever be fully realized even in the example he considers, in painting. In theatre the problem is even more complex, since the act of performance changes along with changing codes. One cannot speak of learning to read an Elizabethan performance the way one can (perhaps) learn to read a quattrocento painting, because all such performances disappeared as they were given. The performance does not come into our culture like the painting, as an external object to be understood, but if it is to exist for us at all must be created again, from within our own culture and using the tools of our own culture, with correspondingly far greater risk that the product will in fact ultimately be a reflection of our culture rather than of its own.

This has not prevented certain theatre directors, especially after the increase in historical research during the nineteenth century, to attempt the detailed reconstruction of past performances. On stages created to reproduce, as closely as historical knowledge would allow, the classic Greek theatre, the Elizabethan public stage, or the theatre of Molière's time, productions have been mounted according to current scholarly theories about the performance conditions of these periods. This approach, although still occasionally encountered, has lost much of the support it enjoyed early in this century, when the problems of its implementation were not so clear. Each new generation of scholars seems to arrive at a new idea of what Shakespeare's Globe Theatre, for example, actually looked like; and in other, equally critical areas, such as the reconstruction of acting styles, the task seems quite hopeless. The problem in any case is not just one of the inadequacy of historical information, but of the phenomenology of performance itself. Even if we possessed the sort of documents about which theatre scholars dream—documents which would inform us exactly how the Globe stage was built and used, and exactly how Burbage played Hamlet on it—these would not allow us to create a theatrical equivalent to the quattrocento painting. It would not be enough to train a modern actor to use Burbage's gestures and vocal inflections. Unless the actor *were* Burbage, we have still created a phenomenologically different object.

The impossibility, practically and phenomenologically, of re-creating a theatrical event with its original signifiers intact, has led many directors to pursue an alternative strategy. Recognizing that much of the semiotic structure of historical performance has been lost, they make no attempt to recreate the original experience or something closely akin to it by reproducing the original signifiers, but attempt to find new signifiers within our own cultural codes which will create new signs evoking the original signifieds. Perhaps the best-known example of this process may be seen in various "modern dress" performances of Shakespeare. When nineteenth-century historicism first began to affect Shakespearian production, directors such as Kean and Booth devoted considerable effort to putting the actors in authentic historical costume reflecting the period in which the plays were presumably set. Subsequently other directors, such as William Poel, aware that Shakespeare himself did not follow this practice, but costumed his characters essentially in the garb of his own time, produced the plays with actors in Elizabethan dress and surrounded them, for good measure, by other seated figures also in Elizabethan dress, following those scholars who have argued that some aristocratic patrons sat on stage in Shakespeare's time.

The result of such experiments often was considerable confusion, due to the great difference in modern performance codes. The spectators on stage were taken to be actors (and in fact were actors, since Poel did not ask any spectators to put on Elizabethan dress), and the appearance of characters from all manner of geographical locations and historical periods in Elizabethan costume ran counter to nineteenth-century expectations of historical verisimilitude. Other directors took a seemingly very different approach, but one with a similar historical orientation. Rather than reproducing specific costume signs, like those of the Elizabethan theatre, they sought to reproduce the code generating those signs, according to which characters from other historical periods were costumed as if they were contemporary to the viewing audience. There is no doubt that this strategy often clarified the signification of costume. When Malvolio, for example, appeared as an English butler instead of an Elizabethan steward, the folly of his romantic pretensions to the lady of the house became much more clear.

"Modern-dress" Shakespeare has itself, however, become a victim of changing performance expectations. After a strong vogue in the 1930s and 1940s it faded and is rarely encountered today. And even when most popular, it clearly created at least as many problems in the interpretive process as it resolved. Hamlet in modern dress may at first seem more immediate, more intelligible, but what does one then do about all the anachronistic language? Are the swords replaced with pistols (in some productions, they have been), and if so, how is Hamlet's death managed? Several years ago a modern-dress version of *Tartuffe* portrayed Tartuffe as an American religious revivalist dominating a contemporary family. This indeed created a kind of contemporary tension, recalling the play's original effect in Molière's France, but created major, and perhaps insoluble, problems of adjustment in the play's other semiotic structures. Since Louis XIV could hardly emerge as the deus ex machina in a contemporary American household, the present state governor was used, and the conclusion thus was vastly altered. What began as an attempt to substitute modern signs bringing us closer to Molière's signifieds ended by distancing us further than a more traditional approach might have.

During the 1930s Stanislavski proposed a more flexible approach to the interrelationship between the presumed semiosis of the original play and that of the modern interpretation by suggesting that any coherent play was given coherence by a "through line of action"—a series of events not unlike the "action" proposed by Aristotle as the basis of a drama, and that any number of specific performance interpretations, what he called "tendencies," could be united with this "through line" so long as they were generally compatible with its own structure. Some version of this attitude is still frequently encountered, both within and outside the theatre, since it seems to offer a comforting assurance of a measure by which we can readily determine what interpretations are legitimate and which are not. In practice, however, the "through line" divorced from interpretation is not so easy to determine, and when a production with what seems to be an unjustified or incompatible "tendency" fails, the choice of interpretation is almost inevitably blamed, even though it is in fact very difficult to be certain that the failure arose from an absolute incompatibility between the interpretation and some deep organizational structure of the work instead of from insufficient skill in actors or directors in the realization of the new concept.

The vogue of attempted historical reproduction and that of placing classic dramas in modern dress (and in the case of Shakespeare, in a bewildering variety of other periods as well) seems, as I have already noted, to have passed out of popularity. This is partly because their novelty became exhausted, but also, I would argue, because more recent ideas in semiotics and reception theory have eroded confidence in the goal which lay behind them and which, though in subtler form, lies also behind Stanislavski's uniting of tendency with through line. This was the goal of recreating something extremely close to the original performance experience. In traditions where revivals of historical work are common (not, alas, in much of the professional American theatre), the assumption is now widespread that the power of these works lies not in a particular set of messages left in them by their originating artist, but by the ability of these works to remain open to the constantly shifting interpretive demands of new cultural situations. Having discovered early in this century that Shakespeare was a Freudian before Freud, then that he was an existentialist before Sartre, and then that he was an absurdist before Beckett, we now have reason to expect the discovery of a new Shakespeare by each new literary movement. We have also increasingly come to accept the fact that this protean quality is among the most powerful and distinctive features of the theatre as an art. What seemed to some theorists of the nineteenth and early twentieth centuries the great shortcoming of performance—its tendency to foreground the semiotic openness of a work of art through constantly varying physical interpretations—has in the modern theoretical context made performance potentially one of the richest and most rewarding areas in the arts for exploring the interplay of art and culture.

NOTES

1. Clifford Geertz, *Local Knowledge* (New York, 1983), 99.
2. Michael Baxandall, *Painting and Experience in Fifteenth Century Italy* (London, 1972), 40.
3. Everard M. Upjohn, *et al.*, *History of World Art* (New York, 1956), 203.

4. Charles and Mary Lamb, *Works*, ed. E. V. Lucas, 5 vol. (New York, 1903), 2:11.

5. J. W. von Goethe, "Shakespeare ad Infinitum," trans. R. S. Bourne, in *Shakespeare in Europe*, ed. Oswald LeWinter (Cleveland, 1963), 59.

6. Peter Brook, *The Empty Space* (New York, 1968), 38.

7. Tyrone Guthrie, "Directing a Play," in *The Director in a Changing Theatre*, ed. J. Robert Wills (Palo Alto, 1976), 89–90.

8. Anne Ubersfeld, *Lire le théâtre* (Paris, 1977), 24.

9. Luigi Pirandello, "Theatre and Literature," trans. Herbert Goldstone, in *The Creative Vision*, ed. H. M. Block and Herman Salinger (New York, 1960), 111.

10. Antony Sher, *Year of the King,* (London, 1985).

Index

Actants, 4, 29, 100–101
Acting, roles, 16–17
Albee, Edward, 26, 34–36
Antoine, André, xv, 78, 100
Archer, William, 62, 118
Architectural semiotics, 42–47, 53–54, 63–73
Aristotle, xv, 6, 26
Austin, James, 32

Balázs, Béla, 102–103
Barthes, Roland, xii–xiii, 9, 47–49, 96–97
Baxandall, Michael, 111, 113–14, 118
Baylis, Lilian, 57, 68–69, 72
Bayreuth theatre, 45, 79
Bazin, André, 79
Beckett, Samuel, 21, 23, 115
Beerbohm-Tree, Herbert, 78
Belasco, David, 77–78
Bennett, Tony, 14
Bentley, Eric, 63
Bergman, Ingmar, 98, 101, 103
Bergson, Henri, 106
Boal, Augusto, 8
Bogart, Anne, 89
Bogatyrev, Petr, 6, 106
Booth, Edwin, 78, 119
Bread and Puppet Theatre, 80
Brecht, Bertolt, 97
Broadway theatres, 50, 59
Brook, Peter, 20, 23, 80, 116
Brustein, Robert, 85, 88
Büchner, Georg, 114
Buckingham, George Villiers, Duke of, 88
Bullough, Edward, 77, 80, 89
Burroughs, Watkins, 65
Buyssens, Eric, xiii–xiv, xvi–xvii, 42

Cabanal, Rudolph, 65–67, 71
Cage, John, 7
Chekhov, Anton, 23, 102
Cody, William F., 85
Cole, David, 96
Coleridge, Samuel Taylor, 89
Comédie Française, 16
Commedia dell'arte, 16, 32–33
Cons, Emma, 68–70, 72
Cooke, Thomas B., 34
Covent Garden theatre, 16, 52, 57, 71
Coward, Noel, 23–24
Croce, Benedetto, 117
Culler, Jonathan, 3

Da Vinci, Leonardo, 112, 116
Daly, Augustin, 50, 78, 81

Dance, George, 67
Darnton, Robert, 85
Davidge, George, 60
Derrida, Jacques, 115
Dessoir, Max, 42
Destouches, Nericault, 35
Dickens, Charles, 61
Dilthey, Wilhelm, 111
Drottningholm, 88
Drury Lane Theatre, 52, 57, 65, 71
Dryden, John, 30–31

Eco, Umberto, 5–8, 12–14, 43, 77
Egeria, 85–86
Elam, Kier, xii, xiv, 76
Elizabethan theatre, 11, 48, 59, 69, 78, 118–19
Environmental theatre, 44, 80–81
Evreinov, Nikolai, 86, 90
Ewell, Tom, 21

Farquhar, George, 34
Feydeau, Georges, 34
Film and theatre, xvii, 79, 81, 84, 102–103
Fischer-Lichte, Erika, xii
Fish, Stanley, 13–14, 16
Fletcher, John, 82, 88
Framing, 7–9, 83, 89
Frederick the Great, 52

Gadamer, Hans-Georg, 113
Garnier, Charles, 46
Gatti, Armand, 87
Geertz, Clifford, 110–112, 118
Genre, 12, 14–16
Geoffroy, Jean-Louis, 22–23
Gielgud, John, 88
Goethe, Johann Wolfgang von, xi, 81–83, 97, 116
Gogol, Nikolai, 104–106
Gottsched, Johann, 35
Granville-Barker, Harley, 62
Greek theatre, 11, 16, 26, 101–102, 115
Greimas, A. J., 100
Griffith, D. W., 103
Growtowski, Jerzy, 80
Guthrie, Tyrone, 69, 72, 88, 116

Handke, Peter, 75–76
Hansberry, Lorraine, 28
Happenings, 6–7
Haussmann, Baron, 49
Hautecoeur, Louis, 42
Hegel, G. W. F., 51
Herzel, Roger, 32

Hita, Pérez de, 31
Hollinshead, John, 66
Honzl, Jindřich, 98, 106
Hugo, Victor, 14–15, 83–84, 86–87, 115

Ibsen, Henrik, 6, 29, 98, 118
Iconicity, xiv, 75–90
Index, 88
Indian theatre, 12
Ingarden, Roman, 115
Innaurato, Albert, 28
Ionesco, Eugène, 80–81
Irving, Henry, 78, 81
Isaac, Winifred, 62
Iser, Wolfgang, 11, 13–14

James, William, 9
Japanese theatre, 11, 17
Jarry, Alfred, 14
Jastrebova, N., 42
Jauss, Hans Robert, 11, 13–14
Jonson, Ben, 34

Kantor, Tadeusz, 106
Kean, Charles, 78, 119
Kerr, Walter, 23
Killigrew, Thomas, 35, 37
Kingsley, Charles, 61
Kirby, Michael, xvi, 3–9
Kitto, H. D. F., 101
Knight, Charles, 61
Kowzan, Tadeusz, xi, 15
Krizanc, John, 84

La Fayette, Mme de, 31
La Scala, 45
Lahr, Bert, 21
Lamb, Charles, xi, 96–98, 107, 116–17
Leo, Jamie, 89
Lessing, Gotthold, 22, 35
Lillo, George, 11
Lincoln Center, 50
Lippmann, Matthew, xiii–xiv
Living Theatre, 85
Lynch, Kenneth, 47–48, 52

McConachie, Bruce, xvi
Marinis, Marco de, xi, xiii, 12, 14, 95
Medieval theatre, 34–37, 85, 89
Metropolitan Opera, 19, 45, 50
Metz, Christian, 79
Meyers, Patrick, 78
Miller, Arthur, 115
Mirvish, Ed, 70–73
Mitterrand, François, 49
Molière, 32–33, 35–36, 47, 85, 88, 118, 120
Morley, Robert, 69
Morley, Samuel, 67
Mounin, Georges, 5–6
Mozart, W. A., 107

Mukařovský, Jan, 98
Mydlack, Danny, 89

Naming (Onomastics), 26–38, 57–58
National Theatre (London), 50, 58, 62–63, 70
Natyasastra, 17
Nestroy, Johannes, 34
New York Times, 19–20, 23, 82

Oklopkov, Nikolai, 80–81
Old Vic Theatre, xvii, 56–73
Olivier, Laurence, 72, 88
O'Neill, Eugene, 28, 98
Open and closed texts, 12
Opéra, Paris, 46, 48–49, 51

Pastoral Players, 82
Pavis, Patrice, xii–xiii, 103
Pearce, John, 68–70
Peguy, Robert, 103
Peirce, C. S., xv, xvii, 5, 75–76
Phenomenology, xv, 7, 79, 81, 96, 102, 119
Pirandello, Luigi, xi, 27, 85, 88, 107, 117
Pixérécourt, Guilbert de, 30
Plautus, 33–34
Poel, William, 119–20
Polti, Georges, 100
Pörtner, Paul, 27
Postlewait, Thomas, xvi
Prague Linguistic Circle, xi, 6, 98
Programs, theatrical, 18–20
Propp, Vladimir, 4, 100

Racine, Jean, 29–30, 47, 84
Reader-response and reception theory, xii, xvi–xvii, 10–24, 99–108, 118–21
Re-creations, historical, 86–87
Reinhardt, Max, 80–82, 87
Rice, Elmer, 78
Richelieu, 51–52
Robinson, Jethro, 66
Roman theatre, 15, 32–33
Rotrou, Jean, 88

Sainte-Albine, Pierre Rémond de, 17
Sardou, Victorien, 30
Saxe-Meiningen, Georg, Duke of, 78, 100
Schechner, Richard, 7
Schiller, Friedrich, 29, 84, 115
Schneider, Alan, 20–21
Scholes, Robert, 103–104
Scruton, Roger, 89
Scudéry, Mme de, 31
Sedlmayr, Hans, 42
Serban, Andrei, 23
Serres, John Thomas, 57, 64–65
Sellars, Peter, 18
Shaffer, Anthony, 18
Shaffer, Peter, 19

Shakespeare, William, 11, 18–20, 29, 58–59, 62, 64–65, 68–70, 72, 78, 80–82, 84, 87, 96–98, 100, 102, 104, 106–107, 110, 113, 115–21
Shaw, George Bernard, 96
Sher, Anthony, 20, 118
Sheridan, Richard B., 88, 103–104
Shirley, James, 34
Simson, Otto von, 42
Smith, Baldwin, 42
Smith, Joseph, 86
Sondheim, Stephan, 106
Sound-and-Light shows, 86
Souriau, Etienne, 100
Stage directions, 96
Stanfield, Clarkson, 65
Stanislavski, Constantin, 100–102, 107, 120–21
States, Bert, xv, 75–76, 96
Stein, Peter, 81–82
Stendhal, 46
Strindberg, August, 28–29, 36–37, 107
Structuralist theatre, 3–4

Taine, Hippolyte, 111
Terence, 32

Tomlin, F. G., 61
Turgenev, Ivan, 104
Tzara, Tristan, 37

Ubersfeld, Anne, xiii, 117
Urban semiotics, 47–54, 58–63

Vanbrugh, John, 34
Verdi, Giuseppe, 88
Village Voice, 19–20

Wagner, Richard, 51, 79
Walford, Edward, 60
Whitman, Robert, 7
Wilder, Thornton, 88, 96
Wilkie, David, 106
Williams, Tennessee, 28–29
Wilshire, Bruce, 7, 83, 88
Wilson, Robert, 23
Wittgenstein, Ludwig, 89

Young, Stark, 96

Zola, Emile, 29